Reviews

Thoughts from educators doing the holy work, on the ground, about *Kids These Days:*

> *Dr. Jody Carrington provides a passionate, powerful, and practical plan that we can all incorporate into our lives starting now. The love and dedication poured into every story, every page, every chapter inspires us to want to do better and be better for ourselves and for the kids we hold dear. If any "kids these days" are lucky enough to have an educator or leader in their life who has the courage and compassion to pick up this book, read it, and put into place the strategies that Dr. Jody so graciously provides us, they are going to be more than ok. This is a book that will challenge you to become the game-changer you were meant to be.*
> —Laurie McIntosh, Elementary School Teacher extraordinaire, Kindness Capes Creator, *Ellen Show* recognized

> *Dr. Jody Carrington nails it in* Kids These Days. *It's a game-changer. Finally, after 25 years in education, I have found a book that speaks to the heart about the important work of educators. Not only is it informative but funny and inspiring. It reminds us how important we are and of the power that we have to change lives. Educators at all levels are reporting a dramatic increase in school violence and mental health concerns. Dr. Carrington provides a practical framework for addressing these challenges and reminds us our students don't stand a chance unless our staff are okay.*
> —Darlene Ferris, Director of Wellness, Wild Rose School Division

The ideas of Dr. Carrington have changed the way our school division operates, and beyond that, how we interact with each other daily. This is not "another thing," it is the thing.
—Paul Corrigan, Assistant Superintendent, Elk Island Catholic School Division

For a reminder of what education can be, read Dr. Jody Carrington's book Kids These Days. *She captures the truth that little can change the trajectory of a child's life more thoroughly than a remarkable teacher. Leveraging the mindset and strategies she shares has the power to transform culture and inspire us to keep changing the world.*
—Dr. Reagan Weeks, Assistant Superintendent, Prairie Rose School Division

Never before have we had a single book that will change the face of education. Kids These Days *provides a systematic, logical approach to lifting up people who hold our children. This investment is the best gift we can give our students for the future.*
—Michael McMann, Superintendent Fort Vermilion School Division

Dr. Carrington provides insightful and practical ideas for educators and leaders that are designed to help them with "kids these days." Through seasoned experience and engaging stories, she makes a compelling case as to why adults need to connect with our kids to help them learn and change their lives for the better forever.
—Kurt Sacher, Superintendent (CEO) Chinook's Edge School division, CASS (College of Alberta School Superintendents) President 2018-19

Kids These Days

Kids These Days

A GAME PLAN FOR (RE)CONNECTING WITH THOSE WE TEACH, LEAD & LOVE

Jody Carrington, PhD

Kids These Days: A Game Plan for (Re)Connecting with Those We Teach, Lead & Love
© 2020 by Jody Carrington, PhD

This book is available at special discounts when purchased in quantity for use as premiums, promotions, fundraisers, or for educational use. For inquiries and details, contact the publisher at books@impressbooks.com.

Published by IMpress, a division of Dave Burgess Consulting, Inc.
ImpressBooks.org
daveburgessconsulting.com

Cover design: Dr. Milena Radzikowska
Photograph of Jody: Leigha Graf
Proofreading & editing: Dr. Scharie Tavcer
Indexing: Dr. Susan Liepert
Book design: Chris Shaddock

LCCN: 2020931589
Paperback ISBN: 978-1-948334-21-1
Hardcover ISBN: 978-1-948334-23-5
Ebook ISBN: 978-1-948334-22-8

First Printing: February 2019
Second Printing: January 2020

IM

This is for you. All of you.

My sweet Aaron and the three we created. We have built a life that I cannot wait to step into every day, and more importantly, come home to every night. This happened only because you all are in my corner.

My mentors—in the early days—Holly Nordstrom, Dwayne Heinsen, John Baynes, Dr. Cannie Stark, and Paul Oliphant. Five game changers who will likely never appreciate their impact.

My team—my Marti, my Kershia, my Dana, my Leigha, my Two Hot Soups. How we came together, only the universe knows. And I am forever grateful.

The three best educators who educated me about education—the amazing Darlene Ferris, Dr. Reagan Weeks, and Paul Corrigan. You three have guided every step of this process. I am forever in your debt. And to Jimmy Casas, for reading this book and writing the foreword—I can't wait to see how we can change the face of education in North America.

My editor and friend Scharie Tavcer, my gurus—the Book Mama herself Linda Sivertsen and my coach and fearless ass-kicker Rhonda Britten. Only you know the blood, sweat, and tears—and pushed me forward anyway.

Last but not least—those who raised me to be this sweary-feisty-funny feminist: My sweet mama, my dedicated dad, my baby brother, my late-to-the-game and still awesome older sister. My three sisters, before I knew I had a real one: Leigha, Tannis, and Rhea. My roots keep me grounded. I got here because of you. Beyond grateful. All ways. xo

PS: To every sweet educator on this planet. This one is really for you. I will, until the end of my career, speak up for, fight for, dream with, and love on each and every one of you who will have me. Because you love on our babies. You dance for nobody every single day. I see you. And that, to me, is holy work. Enjoy.

Contents

CONTENTS

FOREWORD

I still remember sitting on the edge of the couch and looking at my wife with tears in my eyes. The palms of my hands were pressed against my forehead. I was full of guilt, telling her that I could no longer teach. I'd been an educator for well over a decade and to say I was struggling would be putting it mildly. I was exhausted. I'd poured my heart and soul into my kids, my staff, my team, my career. I was at a breaking point and although I knew it, I was too ashamed to admit it. I had failed. Failed as a school leader, as a father, as a husband.

Like many educators who continue to do this noble work, I was naive to think I could do it all by myself. After all, I had the drive, the ambition, the passion, the energy, and certainly the work ethic to do it my way. How foolish I was to think I didn't need anyone's help. Early on I was committed to do whatever it took to find success in my work, but I was paying a heavy price. Both my health and my family suffered and yet I ignored it, because after all, I was committed to the students and to my staff. In my work today coaching teachers and principals in school districts across the United States, I encounter educators every day who aspire for greatness. Not just for themselves, but more importantly, to provide hope and inspiration for others so they too can experience being a part of something great. To never settle for "good enough." And yet, there I sat on the edge of the couch ready to walk away from the very work I always wanted to do.

How did I get there, you ask? Truth? No one was taking care of me, including, well . . . me.

If you are still reading this foreword, maybe, just maybe, it's because you get it. You've been there. You've experienced these same feelings. You know them. You used to be the educator who was making a difference in the lives of babes. What happened? Have you reached a point where you are praying for a snow day just to catch your breath? Or worse yet, like me, have you reached the point where you're beginning to resent kids rather than cherish them? I'm not judging you. I get it. I really do. No one went into this profession to be average. One day you just wake up and realize you're there. And it's a crappy feeling. Ironically, it can also serve as a great reminder of what many of our kids are feeling every day in the schools they attend: isolation, loneliness, and a complete disconnection from their peers and the adults. So how can we begin to reconnect both students and staff?

In the pages that follow, Dr. Jody Carrington reminds us that we must first look after our fellow educators and our own emotional dysregulation before we can be in the right frame of mind to do that for our children. To our credit, we're often so laser-focused on providing care for our students that we neglect our own needs. *Kids These Days* reminds us that educators everywhere are doing the best they can with the knowledge they have when it comes to dealing with students who are so broken it makes your heart ache. However, most often, we continue to work in isolation and in a manner that is unintentionally disconnected. This book will challenge you to rethink how we provide grief and trauma support to not only students, but also the caring adults like you who serve kids daily. Dr. Carrington not only helps us identify and better understand the emotional and behavioral needs of students, but she also provides specific strategies and steps to support our teachers, administrators, and, quite frankly, our often-forgotten support staff.

If we're going to make the impact we so desperately seek without burdening ourselves to the point of exhaustion, then we must work to create a network of districts working together. Districts who understand their own needs, how to regulate each other, and how to do this with the kids they teach. Next, we must create a standard of practice for mental health care for school districts in order to support educators to continue this important work in a way that inspires them to believe what they are doing is making a difference.

I predict that *Kids These Days* will be a game-changer for school districts and educators who desire to make an immediate impact on the life of a child. For years we have done good work, making the needs of our students our top priority. Imagine with me what that work could have looked like if you had a better understanding of the dysregulation of both students and staff, and more importantly, had you not tried to regulate them all by yourself.

It is easy to fall into isolation in our work as educators. It is even easier to avoid that isolation, as long as you are willing to remember these four critical words in order to avoid finding yourself sitting on the edge of the couch, weary and tired, and asking yourself if it's all worth it. What are those four words? "I need your help."

Is it all worth it? Well, simply put, yes it is! Our children need you. We need you. However, we need you healthy and vibrant and truly believing you, along with your colleagues, can do this critical work. We need this book as a guide to help us get there. I am sincerely grateful that we have passionate people like Dr. Carrington who are committed to this important work.

I am ready to join her. Will you?

Jimmy Casas
Educator, Speaker, Author of *Culturize*

A NOTE FROM JODY

The kids are the least of our worries. Seriously. If that sounds blasphemous in a book for concerned parents and educators (and anyone, really, who worries about "kids these days"), then I am so glad you're here. If you own a kid, work with a kid, or love a kid, you will find something inspiring in these pages. Dare I say game-changing? These words were born from the hundreds of stories of kids, their families, and my colleagues who I was lucky enough to meet as I worked across Canada and the USA. My work took me to "mental institutions," rural isolated towns (my favorite), hospitals, clinics, schools, locked inpatient facilities, and day treatment clinics. And regardless of the location or client, the answer is the same (just like I've heard fellow psychologist Stuart Shanker say): **I've never met a bad kid.** Our kids are okay—more than okay. But ONLY if those of us holding them are okay.

If I could work with anyone it would be educators. They're the ones who have chosen to be in the trenches with our kids. Babies just like my three. There is no other institution that most every child on this planet will, at some point in their developmental years, be significantly connected to. There are many people who get to influence kids, but educators, I think, have such incredible opportunities, every single day, to alter the trajectory of a child's life. Part of the question, as I set out to write this book, was whether or not educators these days are okay. Many of the great ones I have met are in this business because they want to make a difference, and at one point in their career, they were doing what they loved with passion and energy. Many tell me, however, that they're finding it more difficult these days to love what they do as much as they used to. I think it's time we did a better job of looking after these educators, plain and simple. And so, this book is for all educators: teachers, bus drivers, administrators, educational assistants, librarians, administrative assistants, custodians, and anyone who leads, loves, and teaches children. If that's you, read on. xo

> *"Somebody's got to be crazy about that kid. That's number one. First, last, and always."*
>
> —Urie Bronfenbrenner

Kids These Days

PROLOGUE

Having spent years sitting across from brave and vulnerable souls in my office, it occurs to me that we are all on the quest for an answer. "The answer." How to get it right. How to do it right. How to be a "good parent" or a "good teacher." I want to start this book by saying, I think I found it. Yes, I'm making a bold statement. I've found that elusive answer. And it's nothing new. It won't surprise you. It's as simple as it is difficult.

First, last, and in all ways, it comes down to connection. To relationship. To light up with the people we love the most, for the people we see every day in our communities, for the kids and families we teach. It's all about connection. Full stop.

And here's the deal. This elusive answer—the one thing I think would make the biggest difference in the world—we all know how to do it. In fact, we are biologically wired for connection. If we don't connect when we're born, we die. We know, to the core of us, what's required when someone is in distress. See, "kids these days" have never felt more disconnected. They feel so unheard, so isolated, that they're taking desperate measures, even to the point of shooting us or killing themselves. And we're still not listening.

So why aren't we listening? Because we're also disconnected! We have so many opportunities to not have to address each other

1

face to face. It's so much easier to look at a phone than it is to repair a relationship—especially if you don't know how. But we actually do know how to repair relationships. See, as so many brilliant ones (like Glennon Doyle and Brené Brown) have talked about, we're wired to do hard things: To help kids who are hurting. To stay long hours and hear hard stories. To help kids work through trauma. To teach kids who have difficulty learning. But we can only do those hard things when we remember this: **We are also wired for connection**. And sadly, the first thing we do when we get sad, or scared, or hurt, is to put up walls of protection and disconnect (just like kids these days).

And here's the other deal (potentially deal breaker): I'm not an educator. I've never taught in our K-12 education system. The only time I've spent in the classroom has been to observe "bad kids" (while, incidentally, thinking to myself that teachers and education assistants are angels). Here's what I do know: Relationships matter. They transcend time, space, race, and religion, and they're the only thing that can heal the world. It's only through relationships that we teach kids how to regulate their emotions—and if they don't have control of their emotions, they can't learn or connect.

The final deal is this: I also believe when we go through hard things, no matter our beliefs or our background, we cuss and we pray. Sometimes, as Brené Brown suggests, when it's really bad, we do both of those things in the same sentence.

I passionately believe that together we can transform the education system in this world, and so you will find both references to a higher power in these pages and a few cuss words too. This book is filled with my heart and my soul. I can't do life in a meaningful way if I can't have access to both of these coping resources. These, along with a little humor, all serve me well. My intent is never to offend, but it is to be authentic. My intent is to share what's in my heart and to be heard. When we put our most precious resources (our future generations) in small spaces every day, we better make damn sure those souls holding our babies feel supported, loved, and ready to help our kids learn the most important lesson we can ever teach them: how to regulate emotion. If we don't do that soon, if we don't focus on being heard and reconnecting, those babes will keep shooting until we do.

• • •

"KIDS THESE DAYS": A GAME PLAN FOR (RE)CONNECTING WITH THOSE WE TEACH, LEAD & LOVE

INTRODUCTION

I remember the day very clearly. I was sitting in my car, preparing to visit a foster parent and reflecting on how I was just a small-town girl (living in a lonely world) realizing the dream of working with the people who could make a difference in the world.

In the years prior to this day, I completed a PhD in clinical psychology and began my career in a locked inpatient hospital unit with kids and families. In the 10 years I was working at the hospital, I learned from some of the best and held some of the most broken. Then after (finally) finding a husband and having (an impressive) three babies in two years, we moved out of the city to raise those little humans and I set up my dream of a rural private practice. And here I was, lucky enough to be consulting in homes and schools "on the ground," talking about the importance of (re)connection (and how trauma can make it all that much harder).

As I was sitting in my car, preparing to go into the consultation with this foster parent, I heard it on the radio: The tragic story that would (eventually) help it all make sense for me. There had been an accident that day. On a farm. In a town just up the road from where I was parked. Three sisters were helping their dad unload grain. They had been sitting on the edge of the grain truck as farm kids often do, watching the canola empty into the truck as their dad and the neighbors stood near. One of the girls slipped off the side and fell into the grain. The other two, desperate to help, went in after her. Two of them died at the scene, while the third was airlifted to our local children's hospital.

As the words of the reporter filled my car, my heart stopped as I thought about those parents. And then I thought about their community, their friends, their teachers. The girls, Katie (13), Dara (11), and Jana (11), had been a part of a school division I had consulted with over the past few months. I had met their Director of Wellness a few times, so I looked up her number on my phone, trying to decide whether I was trying to be a hero in a time of crisis or if there was actually something that I might be able to do to help. Before I dialed, I thought to myself, "Dammit. I don't know what to say," and "I'm sure they have a lot of resources—who do I think I am trying to help?" Then I glanced at a Brené Brown quote I keep taped to the dash of my car: **"Rarely does a response make something better. What makes something better is connection."** I hit send.

The Director of Wellness picked up on the second ring, which surprised me. I told her my heart was broken. She said, "Thanks," and unconvincingly told me they were doing fine and that she had it under control. I offered my support—I didn't even know how but she must know what she needed, right? I hung up the phone, thinking that they had an incredibly long road ahead and wondered if, by chance, they were actually "fine." Maybe school systems were the healthiest place on earth, where they understood the importance of leaning in to each other during times of tragedy.

I went in and met with the foster parent as scheduled, and when I came back to the car, there was a message from the Director of Wellness. "Please call me," she said. "We're not okay." I listened as she told me that there had been hope that Dara would make it when she was airlifted from the scene; however, they'd just received the news that she had also died. Now, that Director of Wellness (who loved her staff) had to deliver the hardest news—namely, to one teacher who was also a first responder on the scene. "I don't know how to tell him," she said. Except I knew that she did. I'd seen her in action before. But like the rest of us, when it's our own pain, our own people, we forget how even the simplest of things work. "Deep breath," I said. "I need you to order coffee, muffins, hold his hand while you tell him, and open the doors to the school to everyone. Hug everyone you can. Call me in two hours. Can you do that for me?" And she did.

That was the start. I never met those Bott sisters when they were alive, but I think of them often. I learned from them that we're wired to do hard things. That we're wired for connection. The only way we survive hard things, in any way that is intact, is by doing that connection part. This was the start of a road that would help me understand that our kids, our employees, our teachers, the people we lead, the people we love, are only going to be okay if the people who hold them are okay too. In the world of education, kids are kids regardless of division, province, state, or country. There will be the "good" students, as well as the ones who struggle, the ones who piss you off, and the ones who die. But those holding them, I've noticed, have little support for these hard things and are often disconnected from each other. We need to change that. Thus, the foundation for this book, for our work, had begun.

• • •

WHY YOU CHOSE THIS HOLY WORK OF EDUCATING OUR FUTURE GENERATIONS

1

(RE)CONNECTING BACK TO THE BEGINNING

Do you remember when dreams were big, and possibilities were endless? Do you remember the day you decided to become educated in this world of educating others? Maybe it was because your mama was a teacher, or a teacher inspired you, or the opportunity to have summers off seemed cool? Or maybe you didn't get the things you needed while growing up and you decided that you weren't going to let that happen to other kids. You were going to be the light for others—the one you needed and never received. Whatever the reason might have been, let's start there. At the beginning.

Back to Your Why

Tell me, out loud if you can or in your head if you must, how'd you get here? Why are you in this job of influencing some of the most important little people in the world? Simon Sinek[1] suggests that we should think bigger than that: What is your critical purpose on this planet? Not just "why" you are here, but what will be your legacy? How do you want to be remembered?

When I think about your job from the perspective of a mother of three of my own tiny humans, here's what takes my breath away: You get to be with my kid in the run of a school week more than I do. Your relationship with my babies becomes critical. The fact that you give up your days, hours, weeks, nights, for my kids makes me so grateful to you. You lose sleep over someone else's babies. You have likely, at one point in your career, considered adopting someone else's child (until your partner reminded you that you weren't rocking it with your own so another human in the mix was likely not a wise choice). You have spent time worrying, thinking, and doing things for someone else's kids while wondering if you should be worrying, thinking, and doing things for your own babies or the people in your own family. Someone else's kids make marks on your heart that you sometimes wish you could erase. If you do this job well, it's going to break your heart.

Think about the top three kids who you'll never forget. Get them in your head. Those kids, those families you bring up in your mind and in your heart in an instant. That's connection. There was something about them, about their story, and their relationship with you that left its mark. And that's the very thing this whole book is about. I promise you if you can get them in your head, they think about you twice as much. You may never know it because they don't have the capacity to tell you. A connection sometimes (often) transcends words. How were they lucky enough to get you? Those are the ones on whom you've had the greatest impact.

My question to you, sweet educators, is why did you choose this work? Is it safe to assume it's not for the pay? Or for the summers off (do you hate when people say that all the time)? I really feel like you should all have t-shirts that say, "I wouldn't need the summer off if your kids weren't so friggin' bad." But I digress. You, my friend, do the hard and holy work.

Our Next Generation

Alice Walker, in *The Color Purple*, wrote: "The most common way people give up their power is by thinking they don't have any."[2] Sometimes, it can feel like we don't have any influence over these babes, especially the ones who are hardest to reach. But I'm going to talk to you about why that is simply not true.

I want you to think about your biggest mentor. Who in your life, maybe a teacher, coach, your mom, your uncle, your Baba, a thesis advisor, was the person who inspired you? Now feel them in your heart. What is it about this person that comes to mind so quickly? As the great Maya Angelou and others have taught us, "people will forget what you said, people will forget what you did, but people will never forget how you made them feel."[3] Your connection to that person is where the power lies.

Our words are powerful. Conversely, you wouldn't listen to even the most eloquent, compelling, insightful words unless you had a connection to the person speaking them. We rarely come out of the gate with, "I'm going to respect you, you tell me what to think, and then I'm going to decide how I feel about you." It always happens in reverse: "When you make me feel connected to you, I'll listen to you all day long." Think about your biggest mentor once again. That's the definition of a good leader. A good teacher. When you can connect with me, I will do anything for you. That's how you can become the most influential person on the planet or set the culture in a school, when you recognize that especially for our broken babies, very few people connect to them. See, the ones who need it the most are often the hardest to give it to.

So Do We Really Have a Problem
with Kids These Days?

When you ask most people about kids these days (and I have), they often say they're "disrespectful. Lazy. Spoiled. Depressed. Anxious." We even have a term for this lot; we call them Gen Zs. These generations of kids have been the cause of many concerned conversations over coffee, with the general consensus that kids these days don't know what hard work means.

But are they really that terrible? Do they really struggle to the degree we think they do? We have a lot of incredible resources in our nation. In fact, Dr. Stan Kutcher[4] warns us that we don't want to confuse mental distress with mental illness. He cautions against pathologizing normal behavior and to be careful with the words we use to describe the struggles kids these days are experiencing. It's so important to keep things in context. I'm going to do my best to remember that, as I tell you how I see it.

So, what are we dealing with exactly? Close to 800,000 people die due to suicide every year (one person every 40 seconds). Suicide occurs throughout the lifespan and is the second leading cause of death among 15- to 29-year-olds. It is a global phenomenon.[5] In Canada, our suicide rate is the third highest in the industrialized world, higher than both the United States and the United Kingdom.

In a study by the Kids Help Phone (2016), it was reported that one in five teens in Canada has seriously considered suicide in the previous 12 months.[6] That means in a classroom of 20 kids, four have a plan. Let that sink in for a moment: Four kids have a plan. And we also know, the more specific one gets in their planning, the more likely they're going to do it. That reality is sobering. Just as troubling, and often identified as the "cause" of suicide, is mental illness. In 2016, the Mental Health Commission of Canada reported that at any given time, 50% of our hospital beds in Canada are used as mental health service beds.[7] That means every second kid in a hospital bed in Canada is there because of suicidal ideation, or a mood-related concern like anxiety or depression. Never in the ten years I worked in the psychiatric inpatient unit at the Alberta Children's Hospital was there an empty bed. Not one day.

So, at the risk of overexaggerating our mental health concerns, I want to offer a perspective about why it's a concern. See, I believe that kids these days have never felt so unheard, so disconnected. Kids are turning up the volume to get their needs met more than they have ever done before. As I write in this chapter, The Sandy Hook Promise reported that 2018 is the worst year on record for gun violence in schools in the USA. In Canada, although school shootings are extremely rare (a marked discrepancy from other countries, which we will address in the chapter on trauma), various protocols have been developed to identify kids who are most "at risk" for committing such acts. We work hard to identify the kids and the reasons, but I don't think the reason is as complicated as we think.

Getting Back to the Good Old Days

Spiritual teacher and author Marianne Williamson altered the way I think about a lot of things with one single quote: "There's no single effort more radical in its potential for saving the world than a transformation of the way in which we raise our children."[8] It's that single word, "transformation," that hits me the hardest. See, every generation before us has said the same about "kids these days." Do you remember ever being told that "you have no idea how good you have it"? I often remember a version from my parents' generation, involving "walking to school uphill, both ways, in the snow."

Nowadays we gather evidence to make our case that our kids are acting out way worse than we did: "They're always on their devices"; "They don't know how to work unless they have a bean bag chair to sit on"; "They're never on time"; "They are so disrespectful and entitled." My personal favorite: "They show up for important things with pants hanging down so far the crack of their ass shows!" See, when we get concerned about an entire generation, we start to seek answers; we get desperate to explain something that causes us such grief. We say, "It must be the gluten"; "It could be all that sugar"; "It's all that screen time"; "It's those violent video games"; "It's the guns" (let's ban guns immediately); "We need to bring back spanking"; or the old adage, "Kids should be seen and not heard."

I don't think any of that stuff is the problem (in part or entirely). I do think access to semiautomatic rifles is not just unnecessary, but a terrible idea. And I do think we need to get back to "the good old days." Our babies now have so many opportunities that make life comfortable, and I'm so thankful for all of those things. After all, isn't that the goal? I believe, however, that the past had one thing over us that we're losing at a rapid rate: Proximity. Never before have we had so much distance between us—literally and figuratively. In this world of massive technological proficiency, we've become increasingly disconnected. Here's how it's happened.

Think about your grandfather. What was the square footage of the house in which he was raised? Houses were small back then. Rooms were shared by siblings or even generations of family members. How much time did he spend in direct contact with his parents, siblings, and then with his own kids (your mom or dad)? Most houses didn't have a TV. They were in greater proximity to each other than we are today. They often worked together during the day and if they had a disagreement, they had to ride in the truck or walk home together. And they didn't have their phones to zone out. If they had a fight that day, they had to figure their shit out before they went to bed, because they were constantly in each other's space. What's changed so dramatically, broadly speaking, is the square footage of our homes. We text our kids to tell them it's dinnertime when they are in the same house! We send our children to their respective rooms when they're fighting.

And then we spend a lot of time and money wondering why kids are killing themselves; why teenage pregnancies are increasing; why addiction is out of freaking control. I really don't think kids are the problem. I don't think that legalizing pot is the problem. Video games, social media, bullying—none of that shit is *the* problem. I believe that the problem, in one word, is **disconnect**. For the most part, it was what the "good old days" had over us. Proximity. It might be the only thing that was better, but it's the only thing that matters. Because the only way you learn that you matter, the only way you learn how to regulate emotion, to stay calm in times of distress, is through relationship. We're more and more disconnected from the people we love today than ever before. The only way we can teach our babies the most important skill is through connection. End of story. That will not change. No matter what development our world sees in the years to come, what will remain paramount is the need for connection. The need for relationship.

Emotional Regulation: The Only Thing We Need to Teach Our Kids

There is a tall (exhausting) stack of how to "parent right" books, how to "teach right" books, and how to do "therapy right" books (and I've read many). Here's the thing: Most have something credible to advise, but if you have a child, the most important job you have as a parent or educator, above all else, is to teach them something called **emotional regulation**.

Emotional regulation means staying in the window of tolerance[9] (during times of distress) versus not losing your friggin' mind when things get tough or when things get too exciting. And the only way you learn emotional regulation? You guessed it: through relationship. If you don't have a relationship with the kid you're trying to influence and support, all of those parenting books, teaching manifestos, or empirically supported therapy manuals will not work.

So, let's backtrack. Think about what happens when we hear a baby we love start to cry. Our likely response is to pick the baby up to try and soothe her or him. If that baby continues to cry, then often the next step is we try the things we know, like changing their diaper, feeding them, taking them for a drive, having a glass (or two) of wine (after the car ride of course), or we call our mothers. Not surprisingly, we rarely give up after we have tried a thing or two to get them to calm down. For example, we wouldn't say to our four-month-old baby, after we tried every trick we know to soothe them and they're still crying, "Hey baby, you're making a bad choice," or, "Show me when you're ready and then I'll talk to you again." But we do this all the time when they get older; we stop helping them regulate their emotions. The important part, however, is the more we assist our kids in regulating emotion when we are with them (to show them how to do it), the less they will require assistance to self-regulate when they're not with us. **The more you can regulate them in your presence, the less they will require somebody to do that for them in your absence**.

The emotional regulation skills we teach our children will equip them to teach their future children—we are essentially training our babies to raise our grandchildren. Not to add to the pressure or anything, but if you're screwing up your kids, you're also screwing up your grandkids. We often ask children in our classrooms to apologize, to be calm, and to use nice words. But if nobody has ever apologized, stayed calm, or used nice words with them, they can't give that away to others. It's not because they don't want to; it's because they don't (yet) know how to do it.

We do a lot of groundwork during their early years to equip our kids with emotional regulation skills. They have very little capacity when they're babies to do this themselves. And they give us so many opportunities to teach them these skills. Just think about how often your two-year-old loses her mind. By the time you launch their precious little butts out in the world (at age 18 or 24—whenever they'll leave, really), your hope is that they've learned enough skills to stay regulated in times of distress so they can be their best selves. Like, let's say I launch my kid off to college at age 18 and he's sitting in a bar having his first-ever drink and he gets knocked off his chair by a big burly bugger. My hope is that my kid will turn around and say, "Sorry dude, are we good?" versus, "What the EFF dude, you got a problem?!" If emotional regulation is a struggle, my kid is more likely to turn around and punch the burly bugger, no questions asked. That's the difference between emotional regulation and dysregulation. The only reason my kid may have the ability to stay calm and make a good choice is from being taught again and again and again how to regulate.

Fun fact: I cannot tell if you have emotional regulation skills until you are distressed. When you are calm, you don't require any skills to keep regulated, so I don't know what you have on board until you're not calm. Say, for example, you're driving home one day and you're thinking about your stressful job and you blatantly but unintentionally run a stop sign and smash into a passing car going the opposite direction. Minimal damage, no one dies—but it was clearly your fault. When the fella you just hit gets out of his car, you're going to hope to Jesus he had somebody in his world who taught him some emotional regulation skills. You want him to be someone who gets out of his car, checks on your wellbeing, is reasonable, and, although he might be mad, he can still sensibly plan for the next steps. But if the guy you hit has little emotional regulation capacity, he might come out of his vehicle swinging.

All that guy has on board to help him cope with the situation of his car being hit by yours is fight, flight, or freeze, and currently he's accessing the fight option. Again, you can't give away something you've never received. More on this later.

Why Our Classrooms? Why Our Educators?

Here's my why: My husband and I have three babies. Every day we deliver them to educators: secretaries, bus drivers, custodians, librarians, before-and-after-school care providers, educational assistants, and teachers. In the course of a school year, they will spend more waking hours with our babies than their parents—my husband and I. In fact, on average, in one school year, those of you in our education system get our kids for 180 days and 950 hours. And if the most important thing we are to teach our children is emotional regulation, and we can only do that in the context of relationship—you all of a sudden matter SO much.

The thing is, kids answer some very important questions based on how the big people in their world respond to them. One of the first things they figure out is if this world is a safe or scary place. If they have been tended to in a relatively consistently manner during times of sickness or sadness, they will develop a story that, indeed, big people in their world can help them make sense of hard things during times of distress. Think about the top three babes you've had in your classroom you've worried about the most: How would they answer the question, "Is the world a safe or scary place?"

Kids start to understand very early, based on the relationships with the big people in their world, if they need to take charge of themselves or if there's someone more capable on whom they can rely who sets limits and boundaries when they are needed the most. If the adults in a child's world have let them down repeatedly, for whatever reason, guess what they'll decide? They'll decide, "It's up to me to look after me, so don't mess with me."

And finally, the most important question that you, I, and the kids who come through our classrooms will answer, based solely on relationship, is "Am I worth it?" The only way we answer this question of worthiness is rooted in the context of relationship. And this concept of worthiness plagues even the most functional people, right? I want you to think about what was going on in your head when you looked in the mirror this morning before starting your day? How kind were you to that game-changer looking back at you? Do you often say things to yourself like, "Damn girl, looking good for 40!" or, "You're rocking that baby weight, girl!" Maybe not. Even on our best days, it doesn't take more than a comment or a question about our integrity, our character, or our appearance to send us down the "am I good enough" spiral. The point is, this question of worthiness is so difficult to answer even on our best days. Even those of us who have a job, have people who love us, and are very secure about all of that will still struggle with this question of worthiness from time to time. Conversely, you can only imagine how difficult self-worth is to determine for someone who has very few of these positive connections in their world.

Here's the kicker: You cannot teach a kid how to regulate emotion on a whiteboard or in a handout.

Here's why relationship matters most: You can teach them strategies, but you cannot teach them how to regulate emotion unless you show them, unless you guide them through that process.

Here's the other kicker: Kids can only learn how to regulate when they become dysregulated. They need relationship (connection) in order for them to want to learn. You can talk all day long with a calm kid about what they're going to do when they lose their mind, but they will forget those strategies when they become distressed. They will need to rely on you, and other big people in their world, to show them how to do it.

And the final kicker: Kids won't learn from people who they think don't like them. They will learn from your positive relationship with them, which is absolutely critical if we are to teach the most important thing ever to be taught.

See, you can have the best pedagogical plan on the planet. Rainbows and unicorns can be flying out of your whiteboards, you can have bulletin boards that just reach out and touch people. Your budget for Chromebooks can be huge. You can have all of that stuff and it doesn't matter if you don't have the connection with the babies you're trying to teach. And oh, when you do, the places they'll go![10]

Am I Worth It?

Think of those top three kids one more time—the ones you've worried about the most throughout your career, or even the friends of your own kid—the ones who break your heart. How do they answer the "am I worthy" question? See, it's easier to help kids answer this question when they're cute, and they smell good, and they have the ability to regulate their emotions. We like regulation in our culture. Those are the kids who are easy to teach.

Let's think about a student named Taylor. Taylor's the sweet one in pigtails. Mama dresses her in matching things all the time and they bring homemade gluten-free brownies to every class party. And she comes to school every morning saying, "Good morning, Ms. S!" in a cheery tone. Ms. S. responds with, "Good morning. Good to see you, kiddo." And Taylor replies, in her sweet, sing-song tone, "Ms. Essss! We just did some baking. Mom thought you might like a little brownie treat because we just think you're such a good teacher." "Thank you so much, sweetie. Let's take our seat now and get ready to start the day," Ms. S replies. Taylor has some regulation skills. She comes into the classroom calm. We can respond well to this kid and we like her. When she does get frustrated with a task, which doesn't happen often, we have a lot left in the tank to help her make sense of it.

Now think about another kid. The bell rings and 30 minutes later in blows the kid everyone knows—he needs no introduction, but he might be named Jaxon (with an "x"). He comes in hot, one boot on because he had something to tell you right away, so the other boot made it to the boot room, but this boot didn't. He bounces into the classroom shouting, "I caught a Pokémon!!!!!"

How does our Ms. S respond to Jaxon? Like right then in the moment, when she has a lesson plan to begin, when the other kids are finally quiet, but this kid, again, arrives late. Some have told me it looks a little like a reckoning. There are a thousand thoughts running through a teacher or an EA's head—most often, "I need to teach this kid how to respond appropriately," or, "This behavior is not a good choice and shouldn't be rewarded" (my personal favorite). All of those responses are valid, and they fuel our Ms. S to respond something like, "Uh, uh, uh, uh—Jaxon. Look at me. Are you making a good choice right now? That is not how you enter our classroom. Where do your boots go? No, no, no, it's not Pokémon time is it? No, it's not. Everybody, is it Pokémon time? No, it's not Pokémon time. Now put your boot back in the boot room and march back to class as quickly as possible. You understand me?" We might also tell him things like, "You're in the red," with the hope that it'll draw attention to his deficits and he will all of a sudden remember the skills he's not (but should be) using.

In an effort to help this sweet boy regulate, with the best of intentions, how does he end up answering that question, "Am I worthy?" Taylor is on time and regulated; she has stories of baking and we want to hear her stories all day long. This guy Jaxon is so excited he got a Pokémon. That's his story today. It's so important to him; however, he has very little capacity to share his excitement in a regulated way, because what he lacks most is regulation skills. And this is how he approaches most conversations. In turn, this is also how most people respond *to* him. Is it appropriate that he's 30 minutes late and he's disrupted your classroom? No. It's not okay. Here's the kicker though—**it's not IF I'm going to direct this kid, it's WHEN and it's HOW**. That's where the magic happens. We will talk all about how to do that in the chapters to come.

Is All Connection Equal?

There is the assumption that because we have the capability to instantly connect with each other via our phones and social media—anytime, day or night, from anywhere in world—that we should know we matter.

Dr. Susan Pinker summarized in her recent book *The Village Effect*,[11] that nothing can replace in-person, face-to-face connection. In fact, specific physiological changes happen in your body in person that cannot be replicated via text or email: an increase in your oxytocin and dopamine (the feel-good hormones) and a decrease in your cortisol (the stress hormone). Just by being near the people you love, there are changes in your body that help you regulate. Have you ever been away from your people when something bad happens? Even if you cannot change the situation, you just want to get home, right? Or you sleep better when the people you love are safely tucked in at home? There is an importance to physical connection that co-regulates each of us to a greater degree than when we are apart from each other.

What we know for sure is that **we are wired to do hard things**. In order to do those hard things to the best of our capacity, we have to remember this: **We are wired for connection**. It is through physical connection with other people that we are much better able to handle hard things. To persist. To be resilient. To remember our "why."

CHAPTER ONE

Game Plan Highlight Reel

1. Why did you choose this profession of teaching our babies? When dreams were big and possibilities were endless, remember those reasons; write them down and feel them in your soul. Remembering your critical purpose, particularly when you're in the trenches, can make all the difference.

2. Kids these days have just as much potential as we all did; however, never in the history of the world have kids felt more disconnected and unworthy than they do right now.

3. The "good old days" had proximity over us—it might be the only thing they had over us, but it's the only thing that matters.

4. Proximity—face-to-face connection—is the only way we teach our children the most important lesson they will ever be taught: how to regulate emotion. They cannot learn anything else when they are dysregulated; it needs to always be our first order of business.

5. You can't tell a kid how to "calm down"; you have to show them. And kids don't learn the things we want them to learn from people they don't like.

So, educators, if you ever doubted the importance of the profession you chose or your place within it, I hope with this first chapter, you are starting to believe that the work you do is holy. Your influence can be endless. We parents need you to know that. If you want to be reminded just how you change lives, read on.

CHAPTER ONE

(Re)Connecting Back to the Beginning

Whether you're a parent or an educator (or both, you amazing soul), here are some things I want you to ponder after reading through this first chapter.

1. What is your critical purpose on this planet? Why are you here?

2. What does emotional regulation mean, and how does it matter in the context of education?

3. Think about the educator, coach, or mentor who had the biggest influence on you. Write down their name. If you can, connect with them and tell them about their impact on you. If they are no longer on this planet, write them a note and send the words up (burning it is a rather aggressive, yet powerful, option). Share what you remember most about the person who inspired you most. In the way you show up today, would you make them proud?

HOW EMOTIONAL REGULATION WORKS AND WHY IT'S THE KEY TO CHANGING THE WORLD

2

TAMING THE CRAZY BY GETTING CRAZY

Fellow psychologist Stuart Shanker said that despite having assessed and treated over 1,000 kids, never, not one time, did he meet a bad kid.[12] Not one single time. These words resonate so deeply for me, for I too have assessed and treated hundreds of kids across the country and never once have I met a bad kid. I have searched through many articles and stacks of books on parenting and teaching (I'll reference all the ones I love within this book), and the ones that make the most sense to me simplify "the answer" universally as: *If you want to have the most influence over a kid, as often as you can, give them your curious and undivided attention, first. And THEN you teach.* It's as simple as it is complex, which is why I think it's so easy to forget. This isn't new, or revolutionary.

How to help our children learn to "make good choices" and be the best humans they can be has been a historical struggle for all of us trying to raise and grow children. And here we find ourselves once again wondering about the future of kids these days. Just for fun, let's back it up and start from the beginning.

Where It All Went Wrong: Behaviorism

Many of us are fascinated by human and animal behavior. In fact, some people devote their lives trying to figure out why it is that people and animals do what they do. During the first half of the twentieth century, John B. Watson was one such person who developed the theory he called *methodological behaviorism*.[13] In his theory, Watson rejects introspective methods and seeks to understand actions by only measuring observable behaviors and events. In the 1930s, B. F. Skinner came along and said, wait a second—thoughts and feelings play a role here too. He called these insights *radical behaviorism*.[14] While Watson and his buddy Ivan Pavlov investigated the stimulus-response procedures of classical conditioning, Skinner assessed the controlling nature of consequences and the mechanisms that signal behavior, calling this *operant conditioning*.[15] Skinner's position (essentially a philosophical one) gained strength with his successful experiments with rats and pigeons that used a lever-press to demonstrate just how powerful rewards and consequences can be, even with vermin. Responses are not just reflexes, Skinner discovered, but beings can control behavior.[16]

Traditionally, behaviorism focused on one particular view of learning: A change in external behavior is achieved using rewards to shape responses of the learners. Desired behavior is rewarded, while undesired behavior is punished. It worked seamlessly for rats and pigeons. Pavlov furthered our hope that we had found the answer to controlling behavior when he and his dogs, through classical conditioning, demonstrated that we can predict behavior with a stimulus. If you pair a bell with food repeatedly enough, the dog will eventually respond to the bell alone because they've learned bell and food go together. Developmental psychologists were carefully watching these theories unfold and discovered that this also worked (in the short term) for kids. How amazing, right? We can control kids' behaviors—particularly when they are unruly—simply by altering their external environment: rewarding the good stuff and punishing the bad stuff!

Basically, these guys tried to make sense of how behavior works by deconstructing it—which makes sense when you are talking about rats. Deconstructing behavior works very well when you don't have a prefrontal cortex in your brain. Humans have one of those. Pigeons and rats do not. Turns out, the prefrontal cortex is a pretty important thing to consider. As parents and teachers, however, we were becoming desperate to make sense of our kids' (unruly) behavior. It appeared to work so well with rats and dogs that we decided to adopt the philosophy and we created numerous parenting programs and education protocols based on what we learned from pigeons, rats, and dogs. It's astounding to think about it—we decided that we should create programs that would "motivate" a kid to be kind or "make good choices." If they don't make good choices, we punish them until they remember to be kind! Seriously?! I am going to be unkind to you in the hopes that you will "snap out of it" and in the future, do the exact opposite of what I'm doing to you right now. A contributing problem to strictly behavioral approaches with kids is that often, in the short-term, it appears to work. So, we keep on doing it. I can make almost anyone comply in the moment, if I have a big enough stick. But in the long term, our intended consequences backfire.

See, we can find a kid's biggest motivator and get them to do almost anything. It works for big people too. If I find your biggest motivator—the thing you could least stand to lose—I would have significant leverage to change your behavior. For example, if you were a parent and I knew your kid was one of the most important things on the planet to you, and I had the power to keep you from your child, I could get you to do almost anything, right? For instance, let's say I thought you were too shy. As your teacher, I decided I was going to "teach you a lesson" about how to be confident. So, I told you that you had to get up on stage, in front of hundreds of people, and sing a Dixie Chicks song. Would you do it? Unrehearsed and embarrassed, you would probably say no. Would you change your mind if I said, "Sing, right now, or you don't get to see your kid"? Chances are, you are going to comply. You are going to get up there and belt out a tune, even if you are full of shame or in tears. (If you're doubtful at all about what someone can actually make someone else comply with in the moment, you may want to review footage of Trump's "no tolerance" policy[17] to see what happens when babies and parents are forcefully ripped away from each other.) Back to our scenario, as you walked off that stage, mortified, would you be grateful that I pushed you to do it? Regardless, your first response is likely going to be, "Just give me back my kid!"

Does it work? Yup. I got you to comply, to do what I thought was best (even if my intentions were good). If I knew a kid's screen time, access to his phone, or recess time was his biggest motivator, I could threaten to take that away in order to get him to do his math sheet, and he'll likely do it. Although I got him to comply, when I play like this, I am often not playing the long game. I got his immediate compliance in the short-term; however, the question remains, what does that leave him with? If I get him to do his math sheet one day by taking away his screen time, what will he say the next day when I ask, "Hey buddy, can you sort out all of these books for me?" What do you think his response would be? Potentially, "No way" or, more than likely, "What happens if I don't?" When compliance from people we love or teach is predicated on what they stand to lose, they will never be motivated by respect. They will be motivated by fear. And fear is very different from respect. Mahatma Gandhi's (1925)[18] words have never been more fitting:

*Power is of two kinds. One is obtained by the fear
of punishment and the other by acts of love. Power
based on love is a thousand times more effective and
permanent then the one derived from fear of punishment.*

We often tell people what to do, rather than showing them. We say to kids, "That's not a good choice" or, "Just calm down!" Here's the thing: Never in the history of telling someone to "calm down" has "calm down" ever worked. Telling someone how to behave is never, ever, as powerful or as transformative as showing them what you want from them. Think about the last time your partner told you to "Just calm down!" How effective was that? What was your response? The hope, when we yell or hiss "Calm down!" at someone we love is they will, indeed, calm down. The hope is they might even look at us and say, "Oh you're right, babe, I didn't realize that I was losing my mind. You always know just how to get me to calm down. I'm just so glad that I married you." I can testify that never in the history of my spouse telling me to "calm down" has "calm down" ever worked. But we continue to do this with everyone, including kids, all the time.

First, Last, and Always, It's About the Crazy

One of my guiding lights through this whole process of understanding just what kids these days need has been a quote that found me at just the right time, early in my career at the Alberta Children's Hospital. The quote is from a dead guy named Urie Bronfenbrenner, a developmental psychologist who was one of the founders of the American Head Start Program[19] in 1965. His being dead is important because I cannot tell you enough that the ideas in this book are not new. They are just as necessary. And they will find us again and again until we start listening. Here's what Urie knew to be true 50 years ago:

*In order to develop normally, a child requires
progressively more complex joint activity with one
or more adults who have an irrational emotional
relationship with the child. Somebody's got to be crazy
about that kid. That's number one. First, last, and
always.*[20]

He was talking about the essential component of being "light up" crazy.
An "irrational emotional relationship." You know that feeling when
you haven't seen a kid you love in a long time and then you lay eyes
on them for the first time? They run to you with open arms and you
just lose your mind with joy? That—right there—is the light up. The
crazy. And it's all we need. We never grow out of wanting the people
we love to lose their minds, or to light up when they see us. We can
witness this beautiful moment in airport reunions, on second dates,
and in young children with their best friends. We are so much better
at lighting up in relationships when we feel a reciprocal connection.
The light up remains necessary; however, our willingness to do it
often fades as relationships become more powerful and complex.
We tend to guard our hearts as people we love become increasingly
important to us. As our love grows for them, so does their power to
hurt us. And usually the people who need it the most are the ones
to whom it is the hardest to give it.

For those of you who are married, your task today is to "light
up crazy" with your partner the next time you see them. What
would happen if you came through the door after work tomorrow,
saw that person you married, and said, "Babe! Hi!!! I am so happy
to see you! I know I don't tell you this enough, but I'm so friggin'
glad I married you."

When I ask folks to try this, most people tell me they think
their partner would wonder what is wrong with them, or if they
were drunk ("You're only nice to me when you're loaded!"). When I
tried this with my husband, his first question was, "What did you

buy?" What's sad about this common reaction, though, is that **the people we love the most are often suspicious when we're kind**. I'm going to say that again, one more time, because I think it's so important: The people we love the most are often suspicious when we're kind. That, my friends, speaks volumes about the epitome of disconnect.

This light-up-crazy is powerful, but it's not easy. In fact, it's so hard to light up, especially around the people who need it the most. Or when we're tired. Or when we're chronically ill. Or when work pressures overwhelm us. Or when we feel unappreciated. Or when we feel just done. Which, by our North American standards these days, is almost every day. It takes a lot of energy to light up, and it can be risky too. People don't always respond to our light-up the way we hope they will. Or, if they haven't litup around us recently or often enough, there's not a friggin' chance in hell that we're going to be the first to do it ("I'm always the one who goes first! Not this time, dude!"). With our children, getting lit up all the time is sometimes also a lot of work. They have endless energy! We search for an easier way, or quicker way, to get kids to mind, or be respectful, or make good choices. Purely behavioral interventions seem to be the best and quickest solution.

But what I know to be true is what's necessary for any intervention to be successful, including behavioral interventions, is that a relationship between the rule enforcer and the enforced must be established. Behavioral interventions tended to work so much better in the good old days when there was more proximity between adults and kids. There were fewer opportunities for disconnection when we lived in smaller houses, when home life came with doing chores together for survival and no one carried phones.

Now, without even proximity on our side, strictly behavioral interventions don't work anymore, particularly for the long game. When what we hope to produce isn't just compliance in the moment, but a generation of babes who are kind, respectful, and connected.

See, you cannot take away enough things from a kid for them to be kind. Eventually, the things you're taking away will not matter anymore, because relationship, on a primitive level, will always trump material things. I have heard many times from parents, "I am running out of things to take away from my kid. They don't seem to care anymore. I have taken away his X-Box, his phone, the door off his bedroom, and moved his bed in the hall. This kid still won't be kind!" In fact, we have decades upon decades of parenting programs and educational interventions based on the research that rewards and punishments alter behavior. Here's the kicker: If you have connection when you enforce behavior via consequences and rewards, these interventions can be and are effective in the long run; however, we rarely measure that variable of relationship. When you're dysregulated, any intervention program is irrelevant, because no one can learn in that state, no matter how "strong" or "empirically supported" the intervention. When you punish me for not making a good choice, what does it do for my sense of worthiness? Not only is it not helpful, it's harmful.

Think about how often people light up around Jaxon (the "bad kid" from Chapter 1 who never listens). And how often people light up around Taylor (the cute kid who always remembers her manners). How often does the light-up happen between you and your partner when you're fighting or struggling significantly in your relationship (i.e., when you need it the most)? The people who need it the most are often the most difficult to give it to.

Enter: A Guy Named John

Dr. John Bowlby has been called "the father of attachment"[21] and is identified as the guy who, in contrast to the behaviorists, suggested that relationship might have something to do with simply altering behavior with rewards and consequences. Let me tell you a little story about this guy named John. John was born in 1907 in London to an affluent family. He was the fourth of six children; his father was a surgeon. His story, like many people, inspired his life's work committed to understanding human behavior, relationship, and disconnect.

John's mother, in keeping with the times of the British upper class, was ever-fearful of spoiling her children; thus, she often only saw John for an hour a day, when he was "presented" at teatime. It was said that John spent more time with his mother during the summers, when she was available, but for the most part, he and his siblings were raised by nannies. John often referred to his nanny "Winnie," who was with him until he was four years old, as his mother figure; she was kind, nurturing, and caring. When she left the family, John described this as one of the most significant (of many) losses in his life, and the impetus for him later discussing the critical necessity of keeping children connected to the people they love. He believes this connection to primary caregivers to be most important, especially in their early years. (This is a concept we still struggle with today, often observed in limited visiting hours for parents in psychiatric hospital settings or our broken foster care system that often promotes "no contact" when kids move from home to home.)

I think I would've really loved John; his story sounds familiar to me. He stated that he learned the most while working at a hospital for kids with trauma histories (same here, John). He also concluded that one of the most important things we can teach kids is this thing called emotional regulation (again, I'm all in, John!). As John explained it, emotional regulation to him meant the skill of staying calm in times of distress. He wrote that if children don't learn this fundamental skill of calming themselves in times of extreme emotion, this will later inhibit their capacity to learn, to grow, and to develop healthy relationships with themselves and others. He explained, however, that the only way you learn emotional regulation is through relationship. You cannot learn emotional regulation from a worksheet or by being told the steps. In order to learn emotional regulation, some*one* must do it for an infant and, as they grow, must increasingly assist that child in regulating. Caregivers and educators must co-regulate *with* a child again and again and again, until they get enough practice to do it on their own. Essentially, I like to think about it this way: The more you assist a child to regulate while they are in your presence, the less they will require someone else to regulate them in your absence. As we talked about in Chapter 1, babies lose their minds frequently; that's their job. The job as a primary caregiver is to soothe and help them regulate, as often as is humanly possible—again and again until eventually we give them more time and space to do this on their own.

More specifically, John and later his posse (see Donald Winnicott[22], Mary Main, and Mary Ainsworth[23]) agreed that there are two very important parts of a relationship that need to be in place in order for kids to learn emotional regulation. John referred to these two things as a "secure base" and a "safe haven." This is where it gets theoretical; however, stick with me for a minute.

You need connection, a "safe haven" to fall into in times of distress. This essential component of having a safe place to land paves the way for the other necessary piece: the "secure base" from which to jump off into the world. The "secure base" is where you set limits and boundaries and also send messages of delight and encouragement, cuing your child that they are capable to take on this big old world. You cannot teach effectively unless you have a secure base and a safe haven of your own. It's not all just about lighting up. It's not just about loving them through it, and it's certainly not about giving them everything. There are two critical components involved in teaching emotional regulation, and they cannot be done in isolation. When we have a secure base and a safe haven in place, Bowlby says we develop a "secure attachment" to that other. And it's only in the context of a secure attachment relationship that kids can learn this thing called emotional regulation. The relationship becomes the critical component.

One of the problems is as parents and as teachers, there's so much pressure to do this thing right. So many opinions. Even the word attachment becomes confusing. Bowlby himself wrote he wished he would have called "attachment theory" something else, because attachment gives the connotation that it's all about connection. And the truth is, you need more than just connection for a healthy relationship. That understanding, sadly, didn't get translated well as others attempted to make sense of Bowlby's theories. If you Google "attachment parenting," for example, the results can be frightening and leave many new parents feeling like failures. Wikipedia[24] provides this definition:

Attachment parenting is a parenting philosophy that proposes methods which aim to promote the attachment of parent and infant not only by maximal parental empathy and responsiveness but also by continuous bodily closeness and touch.

Sweet mother. And WebMD[25] offers this:

Attachment parenting focuses on the nurturing connection that parents can develop with their children. That nurturing connection is viewed as the ideal way to raise secure, independent, and empathetic children.

Sweet mother, and baby Jesus.

The nurturing connection is highlighted, but there is no mention of the necessity for the "secure base," the need to set limits and boundaries, or the need to take charge when necessary.

Social media has molded attachment to pertain mainly to the age of zero to two years—the baby bonding stuff. There is widespread (misguided) belief that if you miss the opportunities to teach regulation at age zero to two years, then there's very little opportunity left for parents. Even worse, if you don't parent very, very well, you're also in big trouble. The message gets equated to mean you must have a dolphin-assisted pool birth, breastfeed till they're at least eight, and quit your job so you can either wear them or sleep with them. Also, if you could do things like bake stuff for every single function, don't ever miss a practice, and make sure your kids are in summer hockey, spring hockey, purple hockey, black hockey, dance classes, and basket weaving just to round out the artistic creativity, then you may produce suitable offspring. That's what "attachment parenting" has become for many. It's such bullshit, really. Particularly for sleep-deprived parents who are looking for the answer to their screaming, tantrummy little muffins of love. Here's the kicker: You can do all of those things on "the unattainable list of perfect parenting" and have a beautiful relationship with your baby. You can do none of those things and also have a beautiful relationship with your baby. I know many parents who breastfeed and co-sleep and babywear. I have also met many parents who "sleep train"[26] their babies and use formula right out of the gate. I see parents deployed to Afghanistan for six months at a time who have a much healthier relationship with their children than those who stay at home. **Read this very carefully: It's not about the method, it's about the light-up. Less is more. What we need is more connection. You, just you, are enough.**

When in doubt, empirical evidence always helps to support a position (at least in the world of academia). Turns out, there is a significant amount of research that's served to support the underpinnings of John's (and his colleagues') ideas, the most powerful of which comes when we look at the brain. Enter next a guy named Dr. Daniel Siegel.

Lid Flipping: The Concept that Changed My Life

In my trajectory of learning, Dan came along and helped make it all make sense. Dr. Daniel Siegel is a Harvard-trained psychiatrist[27] who has dedicated his career to studying family interactions with an emphasis on how attachment experiences influence emotions, behavior, and memory. What I love most about this guy is he makes the whole science of emotional regulation make sense. The research evidence is stunning and far surpasses any empirical support for both strict behavioral methods and modern-day attachment parenting philosophies.

He describes the brain very simply, as being broken down into three parts, and he calls emotional dysregulation "flipping your lid." The visual he's created is powerful. Here it is:

Make a fist with your hand, putting your thumb underneath your fingers, wrapping your fingers around your thumb. Hold it up and in front of you. Your forearm represents your spinal cord and your wrist is your brain stem—the primitive parts of your brain.

That brain stem section handles all of your basic functions you don't even think about—little things like making your heart beat and your lungs breathe.

Your thumb (tucked underneath your four fingers) represents your limbic system. Every mammal has one of these deals. I like to think of the limbic system as housing three basic responses we all have from birth that regulate emotion. It's like whoever, whatever created us said, "Just in case no one teaches you how to emotionally regulate, here's three for free you can rely on for your whole life." They are basic, and primitive, and they operate automatically: fight, flight, and freeze. Think about how an infant, with no language yet, communicates when they need something or when they're distressed. They usually cry, hide, or startle. Those are the three limbic system responses they use until we start to help them develop other strategies. By responding, again, and again, and again, to those three responses, we soothe and teach them other ways to get their needs met (e.g., staying calm, taking deep breaths, using words, teaching them how to understand first before being understood [thank you, Stephen Covey]).[28]

Now for the last part of the brain as represented by your hand model. Hold up your fist in front of you again, with your fingers still wrapped around your thumb. What separates humans from most other mammals is that we have a prefrontal cortex that wraps around that limbic system (the thumb). In our hand model, the prefrontal cortex is represented by the front joints of your four fingers, and they sit on top of your limbic system.

Siegel calls this your "upstairs brain." This prefrontal cortex is where the magic happens. That's where all the good stuff lives. Everything you've ever learned in your life is in that prefrontal cortex. Things like how to drive a car, how to tie your shoes, who's on your family tree, how to judge a heifer, how to speak a language, or what the PIN is to your bank card. Further, the prefrontal cortex also contains pathways to very important things like how to use empathy, how to organize memories chronologically, or how to apologize. All of that stuff lives up there. You're not born with any of those skills (just the structure); you must be taught how to do those skills. And when you're shown how to regulate emotion again and again, by "using your words" when being spoken to in a calm voice, or "taking a deep breath" or "slowing down," you begin to have greater access to those skills when you're in distress. The one time we experienced an apology or the one time we coached a kid through using empathy with another person isn't going to stay in there. It takes repeated lessons to form those skills (the neural pathways necessary to sustain those skills). As a child, if your experience was to largely have others respond to you in a calming way, or to apologize when they wronged you, you now have a template or a map to access when you need it.

Instead if, during times of distress, a child is repeatedly told to "Shut up"; "Boys don't cry"; or to "Suck it up"; or if they have been ignored or neglected, then those are the strategies they'll most have access to when they're faced with someone who's flipping their lid.

One of my favorite things to say is: "**You cannot give away something you have never received.**" Essentially, when we positively interact with our children, we're providing them with the skills they'll use when they raise our grandbabies; our next generation. But, if we harm and traumatized this generation, without corrective experiences to heal that harm they'll raise the next generation in the same way (think about intergenerational trauma from Indigenous Residential Schools).[29]

Another example to help understand this: If you travel down the same path again and again when the sun is shining, what path would you use when a wicked storm comes and you need to get home fast? The answer most often is to take "the path of least resistance," meaning the path that's most familiar to you. So, it stands to reason that the more I can assist you in regulating behavior in a calm and peaceful manner, the more access (experience) you will have to self-regulate when I am not there to help you do it. I must be there to help you to do it enough times, however, so we can establish a path in the road (the neural pathway in the brain). And here's the tricky part: I can only tell you how to regulate when you're calm, but the only way you can learn how to regulate is to get dysregulated first and have someone SHOW you how to be calm. **Telling is what we typically do; showing becomes the necessary component.**

Siegel suggests we think about the prefrontal cortex (your fingers on your hand model) as a "lid." When that lid is on, everything you've learned can be applied because your prefrontal cortex is intact. When that lid is on, you can be kind, show genuine interest in things you love, retrieve necessary memories and lessons about how to stay calm when provoked, and people will enjoy spending time with you. You'll remember the little things because you'll have access to that prefrontal cortex.

The job of little people is, essentially, to "flip their lid" so that they can learn how to put it back on and move forward. Their job is to lose their minds a lot when they are little, because they have very few other skills (if any) to use to show us what they need. Each of those lid flips become an opportunity for us to show them how to regulate. Think about your average infant. They give us SO many opportunities to teach them how to do this, right?

It is important to add that being able to flip your lid becomes biologically critical when we are not safe. There are a number of situations in your life where you will not require access to your prefrontal cortex. There will be times when all you want (and need) to use is fight or flight or freeze. For example, let's say you are out on a walk with your family on a beautiful evening and everyone is holding hands and frolicking in familial bliss. All of a sudden, a car comes speeding around the corner, out of control, coming straight for you and your babes. In that moment, you do not need to know how to judge a heifer or what the PIN to your bank card is. Everything you've ever learned suddenly becomes irrelevant. You want to be able to flip everything that you don't need out of the way (flip your lid), and to (re)act immediately out of reflex (access your limbic system; your thumb). In these emergency situations, adrenaline and other neurotransmitters support this process by flipping your lid in a functional capacity, so that you can act to save your family from the speeding car.

What becomes critical for us to understand is the fact that the limbic system has no capacity to learn. The limbic system (your thumb) is fully developed when you take your first breath. It is the only part of your brain that's immediately wired and prepared for fight, flight, or freeze.

The part that can take on new information is your prefrontal cortex (your four fingers). That has to be engaged (yours and your kid's) in order for you to effectively teach a child how to regulate—you cannot teach them how to regulate their emotions until the prefrontal cortex gets back online (when the lid flips down back down). Our first order of business should be to get that prefrontal cortex back online. It is then, and only then, that you can start to teach. This, of course, flies in the face of all we've ever been taught about consequences that must be "immediate" and that a punishment must "fit the crime." The common vernacular is that if you leave too much time before issuing a consequence, the child will forget the lesson and they won't be able to understand why they are paying the price. But the thing is, "Kids do well if they can."[30] None of us wants to be in a state of dysregulation. We get to dysregulation when we have nothing else to use to get our needs met.

Another important thing to strive for is that your babies should be at their worst when they're in your physical presence. Yup, you heard me. Have you ever been in a situation when someone you know comments on what a polite and behaved gem your kid is, which makes you wonder why everyone else gets the best of them? If only they could've seen what that little "gem" looked like the night before when they were losing their minds about brushing their teeth before bed! I often say that my daughter is the epitome of this experience. She's a fireball. I desperately wanted a girl when we were pregnant. After the first one was a boy, and we then found out twins were on board next, before we found out the sexes I made a deal with Jesus. I agreed to be the best mom to our three children (two at one time), as long as he made one a girl. I picture His response as something in the ball park of, "Oh, you want a girl? Do I have one for you!" I have sat through meltdowns with my own daughter that would pale in comparisons to many of the meltdowns I experienced with kids in the hospital inpatient unit. Rarely, however, does our girl behave like that when she is away from us. That, my friend, is gold. This means that she is regulating herself at school, and when at home, she feels safe enough to get dysregulated. Remember that the only way she will learn how to regulate her emotions is to get dysregulated first. I want her to do most of that learning where she feels safest—at home with her primary caregivers.

But how do we teach this emotional regulation? What does it take to get a lid back on? If someone hasn't taught you how to regulate emotion, how do you give away this knowledge? You can't (think back to the intergenerational trauma endnote above). While in the inpatient unit, with many families who come from multiple generations of abuse, neglect, and trauma, we often were asked how we could help parents learn the skills so that they could give them to the children. Without meaning to, we messed this up—a lot. We often came out of the gate telling parents they needed these skills if their children were ever going to change. I had way too many parents say to me something like, "So, you're saying this is my fault?!" Never, ever, not once, did I meet a parent who set out with the intention to make their children dysregulated. And I knew every parent I met was doing the best they could with what they had been given. We wondered how we could help parents gain some insight into these skills if no one had ever given those skills to them. And then we found it.

Circle of Security

The Circle of Security is a concept that found me at just the right time (as good things often do). While at the Children's Hospital, I was struggling to make sense of how to explain emotional regulation to parents. I went to an introductory training put on by one of the founders, Glen Cooper, and there I had my eureka moment. It was finally the thing that made attachment and emotional regulation make sense. These four rock stars, Cooper, Hoffman, Powell, and Marvin, are clinicians who work on the front lines with emotionally dysregulated kids and their families. Their most recent book, *Raising a Secure Child*,[31] is filled with the good stuff.

These four worked with moms and dads who didn't know how to make sense of emotional regulation in their infants, who needed help to make sense of their child's dysregulated behavior. These parents often didn't have support, and they would often blame themselves, or their babies, when their children lost their minds (as all babies do). Most notably, Hoffman and colleagues worked with homeless teenaged moms who struggled to make sense of emotions, because many hadn't had anyone walk through the process with them, to show them how to regulate.

These four took Bowlby's theory (and those of other amazing souls who said similar things) and masterfully created a simple graphic to help it make sense to parents and caregivers. It's a delicate balance to talk about the need for caregivers to be the models for their children while not blaming them as the "cause" of their babies' (necessary) dysregulation, but rather that they are the solution. The premise of their theory, Bowlby explained, is that emotional regulation is the most important thing we teach kids. Any attachment figure can teach these skills to our babies, anyone who is the regulating other in the relationship. And in order for this regulating other to teach this skill, these theorists say we need to be two things for that child: **A secure base and a safe haven.** So, if you're a parent, a teacher, a coach, a bus driver, an aunt or uncle, a grandparent—really anyone—this gives you the opportunity to serve as an attachment figure.

Here's another way to look at it. Consider taking your three-year-old to the park. Imagine you are in the car on the way there, your lid is on, her lid is on, her bucket is filled, and everybody is calm. Parenting nirvana, essentially. As you sit on the park bench, you are the hands on the circle for your babe. She will start out near you and look to you to establish whether it's safe to venture forward. You become her biggest fan. You might say encouraging words, "Go play and have fun, honey." She checks back occasionally for the cues that reassure her she's safe and whether she should go further out to explore. You'll nod encouragement or smile, which is her cue to go out into the world, on the top of the circle.

As an educator, the top of the circle is where you want the kids in your classroom to be. This is where curiosity lives. The top of the circle is where they have access to everything they ever learned because their prefrontal cortex is on. They can look around and start to make assessments about the approachability of other kids on the playground. They can decide what they would like to do first. They might notice the slide and recall how much fun slides can be. They love slides, and off they go to explore the new corkscrew slide. This babe can think of those things because they have access to their memories and experiences with slides and kids their size.

Let's imagine that your child comes down that corkscrew slide and then runs through the gravel to the swings. Suddenly, they trip and skid their knees through the gravel. It hurts and they might be startled. What happens to their lid? It flips. They need assistance to make sense of this hard thing and currently, they cannot do it alone. They will need somebody to help get their lid back on. They come down to the bottom part of the circle and run to you for comfort and support because they're only three and cannot do that on their own yet. They are seeking the bottom hand, their "safe haven," to help them to regulate emotion. You provide comfort and back they go to explore and play.

It's often easy to spot a "flipped lid" when kids are in situations like these because they often respond with a fire-engine-type wail. It's the cue to us big people in their world: My kid's lid is flipped, she's dysregulated, and she's coming back into the bottom part of that circle for my support. As the caregiver in this situation, how do you respond to a child? We welcome the child back into our arms and comfort and soothe her. We might kiss it better, give a hug, or find a bandage (unless, of course, you're a dad from my parents' generation where the theory was "if it's not broke or bleeding, don't make eye contact." Or, better yet, "Spit on it"; "It'll make you tough," which is why I'm still in therapy. But that's a whole talk about miscues we can have in another book). Back to our playground. When we offer soothing connection, the child's lid comes back on, sometimes like magic. This once wailing little mess is now back, wanting to play again, because you've made sense of her distress and her prefrontal cortex, the lid, flips back on. She goes back to the top of the circle, where they explore and where curiosity abounds.

Lid flipping can happen during positive emotions, like big excitement too. For instance, that same little person goes out to explore on the top of the circle again and let's say they find something that's so freaking amazing they flip their lids. They're so excited about what they have discovered that they cannot possibly do one more thing in their world until they share it with someone important. After discovering something that they're sure is a dinosaur tooth, they might shout from the other side of the playground, "Dad! Look what I found!! It's a dinosaur tooth!!" Most often you will inspect said tooth and if you share in their joy, or "delight in them," they will then be able to regulate again. You're fully aware that it's a cigarette butt they have discovered; however, you say something like, "Let's save it and take it home to show mom later." And proudly, after the find is now delighted in and safe with you, off to the top of the circle they're able to go again.

This is a very simplified version of the Circle of Security theory, and Kent Hoffman and crew[32] present it much more extensively in *Raising a Secure Child*. What I find amazing is, now that you know about the circle, you will see it happening everywhere. You will see kids going in and out of the circle in all kinds of places—in the store, at the coffee shop, in the dentist's office. It's a universal process. And we never outgrow it.

The Still Face Project: Further Evidence

With their historic work called the Still Face Project,[33] first presented in 1975, Dr. Edward Tronick (later Cohn and Tronick) taught us that as early as three months of age, children travel around "their circle" (they didn't use the "circle" terms specifically but I'm adopting them here for clarity of concept). In an experiment, Tronick instructed moms to look at their babies, to engage and play for a few minutes. He then instructed the moms to stop the engagement, look away slightly, and go still with their facial expressions. The footage on Tronick's work is compelling and fascinating. What they observed (and recreated a number of times) is babies will start to flip their lids to get their needs met (mom's response) almost immediately after noticing mom's lack of connection.[34]

First, the infant will typically start by making themselves look cute, eyes get big, trying to get mom's attention again. Then, they might start to coo, purse their lips, and point to try and get mom back on track. When mom is instructed to still not engage, her infant very quickly becomes distressed, looks away, gets frustrated and starts to fuss and cry. Essentially, they start to flip their lid more and more intensely, a primitive response intended to reengage their regulating other (mom).

That same experience plays out throughout our lifespan. When you are playing blocks on the floor with a three-year-old, for example, you can be sitting with them, observing their play. Often, as long as you're present and engaged, they don't really need you and will continue playing comfortably. They know they have a lid-flipper-back-on'er available and at the ready, if required. They don't need to sound any alarms.

What happens, however, the second you leave to do the stealth mission of checking on supper in the kitchen or answer the phone? In my house, it doesn't take long until my favorite word is on repeat: "Mom, Mom, Mom!" Way too often I have thought (and said) things like, "Come ON! I have just put in some quality block-playing parenting time, surely you are 'filled up' and enough to give me a minute of reprieve for a phone call!" Not a chance. Children are like heat seekers. When you're otherwise occupied, they can smell it, and they check to see if you'll be available, just in case.

If you're in my house, and the "Mom, Mom, Mom!" starts, I might initially respond with something like, "Liv, look at me. Look at me. Dora is on. You go watch Dora. Mommy needs five seconds. It's very important, okay?" I don't know about you, but not one time has one of my children responded with, "Oh absolutely, mom. I'm just going to put my lid back on and regulate myself over here. When you're ready, let me know." Not once, ever. They don't know how to do that on their own so Liv will say, "Mooooooooooooooom!" then I say, "Can you just listen? Look at me. Here are some gummies, share them with your brothers and I'll be five minutes. Go!"

Now, if you're my daughter, what happens after I get back to the phone, within about, let's say, eight seconds, is she'll find the thing that will demand my attention: a throat punch to her brother. This usually does the trick. And then she has me. Because I didn't meet her at the bottom of the circle (in her mind), she's going to turn it up high enough until I have no choice but to intervene. Then, I'm punishing that throat punch, but, in fact, I missed the cue.

Kids are hardwired to turn it up louder and louder until we meet their needs and assist them in making sense of their world. We need to assist them differently to regulate. When they get language, their cues can get more and more confusing. When they say things like, "Shut up, whatever. Get out, it's my room," we usually don't see those "cries" as we would have when they were babies. When their behavior was "off" as an infant, we would typically persevere until we decoded the cry. When they get older and say hurtful things, however, we have a greater tendency to be hurt by their responses and walk away. Our pull to teach them to be respectful trumps our call to sort out the problem. So, we might say things like, "Excuse me? That's not how you speak to me." Or, "Watch your tone, young lady." Imagine if we said that to babies without language. They are crying. We changed their bum, they're still crying. We fed them but they're still crying. After the third or fourth attempt we say, "Okay, listen. I don't like your tone, young lady. When you're ready to make a good choice, just raise your little arm and then, and only then, will you earn my attention."

I wonder, though, what is that the equivalent of a three-month-old cry in that sullen teenager? Something is not okay with this "babe." We could think, "She is a disrespectful, ungrateful mini human, and we failed her awfully," or we could think, "She's just like her lazy, unmotivated father." Or, we could recognize that she's dysregulated and she doesn't know how to get her needs met.

Just like when they were little, our goal is to (eventually) get her prefrontal cortex back on. Sometimes, as our kids get bigger, they need a little bit of a break first, but it's more about the pursuit of connection that matters. Guess who we give up on the most? The prickliest, hardest ones who need it; the ones who get very good at saying "I'm fine" to everything. Either way, when something isn't right, we need to do our best to figure out what that is.

Here's one of my favorite things about this Circle of Security model. The most important things you need to remember when you're a regulating other is right here, in 25 words or less: Your job as the regulating other will be to **"Always be bigger, stronger, kinder, and wiser. Whenever possible, follow a need. Whenever necessary, take charge."** More specifically, when you're parenting or educating a child (or leading a team) Cooper and colleagues instruct that your job is always to be two hands on the circle—bigger and stronger (the top hand) and kinder and wiser (the bottom hand). Don't doubt it for a second that the big person (or the leader) is the one who can keep you safe and who calls the shots. Whenever possible, follow your child's need. Whenever possible. Those words are the most revolutionary part of this model for me. They mean that when the kid is losing their freaking mind, you need to dig deep into the core of yourself and figure it out **with** them. You know what we do way too much? We take charge. We have a very hard time following their need when they're lying, cheating, stealing, or dysregulated. Our first response, typically, as a teacher, a parent, or a partner, is to fix their distress.

Cooper and colleagues finish their summary of "all you need to know about attachment" by saying, "Whenever necessary, take charge." When safety is an issue, if they're going to hurt themselves or somebody else, then all bets are off, of course. Whenever possible, follow the lead. Whenever necessary, take charge. Having access to the prefrontal cortex—having the lid on—is where the magic happens, and that's what big people have to help little people get back to doing. I ask this of myself all the time as a mom: "Is this a take-charge moment?"

All of this isn't anything you need to do perfectly. We're going to screw this up so much because we've got our own stuff going on, because we're exhausted, because our kids drive us nuts. Or they remind us of our mother-in-law or our father. We're going to lose our minds sometimes and that is okay too. You can follow a need until it's time to take charge. Sometimes you can follow a lead for hours. Other times you may have two seconds of tolerance before you take charge. Often when I talk about this, people reflect on their own parenting fails and I can see the desperation and the defeat in their faces. Cooper and friends suggest "getting it right" or having hands on the circle even just 30% of the time will be "good enough" to teach your child how to regulate emotion. They acknowledge, in their most recent publication, that it becomes very difficult to quantify what is "good enough" to assist your child in learning how to regulate. What is critical, however, is we will all inevitably fail at this. We don't have to be as "perfect" as we might think we have to be. The goal is to do our best as often as possible, and sometimes that will only be 30% of the time. The truth lies somewhere in the importance of following the lead for as long as we are capable on any given day. Where I fall down as a parent most often is when I get worried that I'm not teaching or I'm not educating when my kids are melting down and not listening. And on days when I'm tired, or overwhelmed, I lose my mind a whole lot more. More often than not, it's the follow-the-lead moments where we teach our kids the most. We will not get this right all the time. Ever. The goal is just for good enough, and they will be okay.

Quiet Versus Calm

Another fellow Canadian psychologist, Dr. Stuart Shanker (we are super smart, us Canadians), wrote the incredibly insightful read *Self-Reg* for teachers and parents.[35] He said one of the most brilliant things I've heard in a long time: *"There is a big difference between kids who are quiet and kids who are calm."* In education, there's a long-standing history of developing behavioral program plans to keep kids quiet not calm. Many of these behavior plans are predicated on "motivators" and "triggers" in identifying the most effective way to keep kids from losing their minds. This seems reasonable on the surface. In fact, it seems responsible. When you're the boss of 30 little humans in one room, it stands to reason you want to create the most peaceful learning environment. Keeping the bouncy ones quiet seems to make sense for the greater good.

Here's the thing: You can never really know the complete list of triggers anyone has. Even the most insightful of us can't explain why every time they hear a song, they get instantly sullen, or when they have to do something with no time to adjust, they lose their minds. When we work to try and keep triggers from kids, we're aiming to keep them quiet—to not set them off, to avoid a lid flip. Remember though that you've got to dysregulate in order to learn how to get regulated. The best time to teach (model) the most important lessons of regulation is actually when their lids are flipped. So instead of a plan to keep them from getting triggered, what if we had plans that prepared us for *when* kids lose their mind and less on trying to walk on eggshells, so they don't lose their minds?

CHAPTER TWO

Game Plan Highlight Reel

1. Rewards and consequences alone will work in the moment—especially if you have a big enough stick—but the more important question remains, "Where does this approach leave the relationship?"

2. First, last, and always, it's about the light-up, the "crazy." Don't forget that the kids who need it the most are often the hardest ones to give it to.

3. John Bowlby, the "father of attachment," taught us it's all about teaching emotional regulation first—being both a secure base and a safe haven to those we teach, lead, and love, so they can learn.

4. The founders of The Circle of Security created a parenting model that helps clearly explain our critical role in teaching our children emotional regulation. We have to be regulated ourselves (at least some of the time) in order to teach our children regulating skills.

Having "hands on the circle," at least 30% of the time, becomes critical in teaching our babes how to regulate.

5. The primary job of every child is to do what Dr. Daniel Siegel refers to as "flipping your lid." Kids can only learn how to regulate when they dysregulate first. There's a big difference between kids who are quiet and kids who are calm.

To sum up this critical chapter, it's not about the specific strategies or programs you've incorporated in your school. Every program can be effective (and likely has empirical data to support it); however, a necessary component often **not** highlighted enough is, without fail, the necessity for an underlying philosophy of connection. A relationship to the one you're trying to teach is where all the power lies. It can be a lot to consider, I know. I'd love to share a bit about just how I've come to understand kids these days. You, my dear game-changer, are an important part of the game plan that will allow us a better chance of staying in the game with those who need it most. Read on if you need to find some hope again.

CHAPTER TWO

Taming the Crazy by Getting Crazy

This chapter is all about understanding why the easy part is getting kids to comply. The hard part is remembering that what you leave them with is the most important thing. These words reflect a little behind the neuroscience at play that makes kids (and big kids) tick. Consider these questions:

1. In your opinion, is there room for behavioral approaches when parenting and teaching our children? What might that look like in your classrooms or in your parenting relationships?

2. Share what your "light-up" looks like. Who do you find it the easiest to light up around? Who, right now, in your world, might just need a little more of your light-up?

3. Talk about your understanding of Siegel's "lid flip." How does your understanding of the lid flip help you in the context of your classroom?

KIDS THESE DAYS

3

HOW I SEE THEM

Often times when I'm asked to do a consultation with a school, I can hear the desperation in the voices of the administrators. The conversation usually starts something like this: "Never before, in our collective 58 years of educational experience, have we seen a kid like this. This one scares us." Then I say, "Tell me more," which is often followed by a list of concerning behaviors and any assessments about their diagnostic profile (some have come with diagnoses and others get diagnosed by the staff). Usually, the most concerning behaviors are listed first: The lying, the cheating, the stealing, the lack of remorse, the no empathy, the drawing guns, the spitting, the kicking, and telling teachers to go "F" themselves. Or the more concerning ones (in my opinion), the babes who don't say a single thing, to anyone, ever.

When I was trying to break through the armor of babes who have a difficult temperament, a complex physical makeup, a history of trauma, or all three, here's how I made sense of things. I put kids into three categories along a continuum of insecurity: (1) the regular lid-flipper kids (remember it is their job to lose their minds as often as possible in our safe presence); (2) the Caillou kids; and (3) the Flat Stanley kids. Let me tell you more.

The Regular Lid Flipper

Typical Developing Kids

Here's the deal: All kids should be distressed in your presence at some point. They should seek to be delighted in by you, to get your approval, and they should seek your assistance to ground them in times of distress and excitement. These are the kids who ask you to take a look at their work, and it often takes very little encouragement to "fill them back up" and have them on their way again. These kids are the ones who get mad at each other on the playground and need you to help them make sense of it; they can apologize and move on to whatever is next. That is the circle in action and the perfect opportunity to create a neurological pathway they can access when no "hands on the circle" are available in future situations. Some days will be worse than others, of course. When they're tired, or when they're experiencing additional outside stress, they may flip more often, but you can also get them regulated again. Sometimes it takes a few seconds. Sometimes it takes an hour. But you can get them regulated, particularly when you have the capacity to stay calm.

Caillou Kids

My "Beat Them to the Punch" Babies

Think now about crossing over the proverbial line into attachment insecurity. I like to think of it as a continuum (based on my interpretation of attachment subtypes from some of the greats like Mary Ainsworth and Mary Main[36]).

For me, close to the line of "normal" versus clinical (let's be clear, it's a line in the sand), we have the kids who I like to call "Caillou." If you are not familiar with this kid's TV show, stop right now and pull up an episode on YouTube. It will be painful but purposeful. This little dude—in short, a whiner was often the bane of my existence when my own babies went through a stage of watching Caillou. Rarely is his bucket full and there's always, always something wrong for him.

In your house or in your classroom, this babe is often the one standing at your desk waiting before you can even get your first sip of coffee. You might avoid him (sometimes—like not every day—not in September at least). There's always something wrong: His pants are too tight, his arm hurts, he asks a question about the same thing (100 times), and someone else is always "being mean." These kids never seem to miss a day of school and they are the ones who leave you feeling like you are just not enough.

How do we typically respond to these life suckers? Often, with good intentions, we put up boundaries and we teach them about "personal space bubbles." We set limits, with the hope that they will learn when it is or is not appropriate to ask questions. Or ask for another hug. Or to tattle on another kid. We have been taught for years to ignore bad behavior. It even has a name: "planned ignoring."[37] The hope is that the child will suddenly realize that your avoidance is a clue to what you want from them. Or that they will observe you attending more to other children who can ask questions in a calm manner and the expectation is their little brains will then figure this out and they will start to "act accordingly." But what is very difficult for most Caillou kids is that they're challenged to make sense of cues like ignoring.

Way back when I was in university I coached a kid's novice hockey team, tier "bottom of the barrel" (that's not what they called these six-and seven-year-olds; however, it was clear that I was coaching those who were not yet able to make any other team). I play hockey, love the game, and decided this would be a good idea to get more experience with kids (and potentially make my resume look more impressive). I was not a parent yet, but I had a lot of child psychology courses under my belt, so how hard could this be? And then I met "Caillou" (the nickname I gave this little muffin of love). He was the kid who came into most practices with a complaint. He would drag his bag dramatically into the dressing room and say things like, "Coach Joooooodddyyyyyy, I feel like I have a tummy ache today." After the first shift, often he would ask for water. I would say, "Dude, you have your water bottle over there. It has your name on it." Insert really whiny voice: "But coach, I don't know how to work it. Can you help meeeeee?" So, I would grab his water bottle and shoot him with it, maybe missing his mouth just a bit, with the hopes of "teaching this kid a lesson," thinking maybe next time he would become more independent and grab his own water bottle. Good intentions, but can you guess what the results were? I had a kid who was now bawling because "You got me all wet!!!!" Sweet Lord have mercy.

I also tried ignoring this kid. On the bench, I would give the others praise after a good shift, while this dude rarely knew where the puck was. He'd say things like, "Coach? Coach? Did I do good too?" and I'd say things like, "No. No dude, you didn't do well. You were sitting in the other team's net! Play your position like we talked about in practice." My intention was to get him to realize that if he wanted my praise, he needed to pay attention and play more like he was taught. You can likely guess how he responded to this well-intentioned teaching: He started to sob. "You hate me," or more often, "I hate you! You suck!" Loudly. And when I coaxed him off the bench and back on the ice again, he would lay on the ice and roll around until the referee would look at me like, "Could you do something about this kid?"

There's a popular children's book called *Have You Filled a Bucket Today?*[38] The premise is about the importance of kindness and that when you make other people feel good, you get the best of them. I often think about these Caillou kids as having holes in their buckets—for a variety of reasons—but what they require is (extensive) bucket-filling. Trying to manage their behavior with rewards or consequences is not effective, not until their buckets are filled. But because of the holes in their bucket, it requires us to "beat them to the punch." It requires us to get to them (to fill their bucket) before they get empty enough to have to pull it from you. It's often the last thing you want to do with these kids. But with these guys, a "let sleeping dogs lie" approach backfires.

I realized I had to change my approach with my hockey Caillou kid. So I started meeting him at the door of the dressing room, before he even sat down, and I would say things like, "You're here! I'm so happy to see you!" Or as we were walking to the ice before the first period, I would have his water bottle ready, asking him if he needed a drink yet. And if I could, I would make eye contact first, at the end of every shift, and say something (anything!) that he did right. You can imagine when I started doing this, the kid was suspicious. "Why are you being so nice?" See this is exactly where I want him to be, because then I know he's using his prefrontal cortex to try to understand what's happening. He's noticing my responses, which means he's not in fight, flight, or freeze mode desperate to get my connection. For this hockey Caillou kid, after "beating him to the punch" as often as I could, coupled with relentless asking if he needed a drink from his water bottle, his behavior shifted. By about the second period he would say, "Coach, I'll get my water bottle myself when I'm thirsty!" That, my friends, is a huge win. His bucket was full. His lid was on, and he was at the top of the circle. He had access to the things we'd learned in practice and he could more easily tolerate things that went wrong on the ice (e.g., another kid takes him out or the other team scores).

From my years in the inpatient unit and consulting on the toughest kids in classrooms, I offer you this: From this day forward, every time you hear yourself say, "That kid is attention seeking," try to replace that phrase with, "That kid is connection seeking," and see what happens. Just notice. If we can make just this one change in the way we see the Caillou kids, I think it would significantly alter the capacity we have to hang in there and respond to the kids who suck the life out of you by simply beating them to the punch first.

Flat Stanley Kids

My Go-Low and Go-Slow Babies

As we head down the continuum of attachment insecurity, I want you to think now about the kids whose incessant question-asking has stopped. Or maybe it's never been there. These kids are flat, reserved, unnaturally quiet, and struggle with eye contact. They can appear aloof. Or sullen. They are very skilled at keeping distance from you and others. Marlene Moretti,[39] another of my Canadian attachment-theory heroes, refers to this group of kids as having either "hot anger" (they say they don't care, but you know that's not true) or "cool anger" (when they get even more serious and skilled at actually appearing as though they don't care what you think). You can't hurt them—simply because big people in their world have let them down way too many times and they trust no one. That's how they protect their hearts. It's not because they want to act this way, but they haven't been given other choices. These babies never, ever come without a story that crushes your soul.

I remember what one of my Flat Stanley patients taught me when I was at the Children's Hospital. After numerous sessions of trying to get her heart, the first small crack in her armor was when she said to me, "Don't you know that mad is just sad's bodyguard?" She was twelve and her parents were struggling significantly. She was a beautiful girl who, when calm, was a kid who you could not fathom could master the destruction she could create. She would provide very little insight with what was "wrong" with her, except when she would strip down to her underwear in our secure room and threaten to pee. She would kick and hit and scream. I wish I would have understood then what she was trying to tell me. I worked so hard in my naiveté to reward her when she was making good choices, and to take away the things she loved when she had one of her rages. I saw her, but I didn't listen to her. Something was going on, but we never figured it out. **Behind every mad is a sad**. I've never, not one time, met a mad who wasn't sad. There's always a sense of loss, a sense of something that's not okay, and they're just going to be really friggin' mad about it, because being mad is so much easier than getting to the sad. The tough part, though, is that getting to the sad can sometimes take time. And it always takes relationship.

These kids are those who need us to "go low and go slow." Let's be clear: They have the exact same needs as the Caillou Kids. They have just learned (or have a temperament that won't allow them to learn, or a trauma history, or holes in their brain from a neurological condition), that constant attention-seeking goes nowhere (or earns a harmful response), so they stop doing it. They stop seeking attention. They appear flat, indifferent, or even mad all of the time.

If you're like me, these are the babes who I love to work with; I am desperate to get them "out of their shell" to figure out what's wrong. I'm compelled, more than ever, to "light up" in my crazy way and show them they matter. But they can't hear when messages are big, loud, gushy, or over-the-top because it scares them. It sends them into fight or flight. They don't trust it because rarely (if ever) has anyone responded to them like this, so they have no script for how to respond. They assume you are faking it or that it's a ruse for something sinister. They often get embarrassed and they certainly don't trust it. So, they will either tell you to "Fuck off," or they'll stop coming to your class, or your sessions. They desperately want to believe they matter, but a "go-low and go-slow" way is better. I might meet this kid at the door with a quiet hello. I might leave a note in their agenda or in their backpack about how proud I was of an accomplishment. If I'm coaching a kid like this, I will speak quietly on the bench to him only, instead of drawing the whole team's attention to him. He can tolerate it better this way. He can hear it, because I'm not flipping his lid. And slowly, but surely, he will wonder if it's possible that some of what I'm saying is true. And that's exactly where I want him to be.

These kids are often tough to break. Not always—but often. They require long-term support and reassurance to stay in the game. They are often so hurt that they can be mean, disrespectful, or hurtful in an effort to keep you at bay. They think it's safer for them and for you. Our only job is to teach them otherwise.

A Word on Attention-Seeking, Manipulative Liars

Some kids are referred to as "attention seeking," or "manipulative," or "liars" in some consultations or team conferences I've had. Often these descriptors were used to draw attention to just how worried the adults were about the state of that kid. It often reflected a place of exhaustion and concern that nothing was working. These kids can be a Caillou or a Flat Stanley, but the big people are trying to make sense of the kid's behavior and often see their lying, cheating, or stealing as "manipulative." These kids might say things like, "I went to Disneyland last night, Ms. S." How do we typically respond to what we know is not true? Our approach is so pure and honest— we want to teach them that lying is not a good tactic. So, our noble attempts at correction often look and sound like, "Hey, hey, hey, hey, hey. You and I both know that's not the truth. We tell the truth in here. Isn't that right? When you're ready to tell me the truth, then I will be ready to listen." Our intention is fantastic. We want to teach them lying is not okay. Is this a take-charge moment? You get to decide that but, oftentimes, when we take charge we miss the point.

The point is that we forget to ask why. Why are they lying, or making up stories, or trying to "manipulate the situation"? Let's think about all the possibilities: Maybe there's something wrong with this one's brain? Maybe they're growing into a psychopathic serial killer? Maybe it is genetic and there's nothing we can do about it? Or maybe they're lying to protect themselves? You and I sometimes lie to save face, don't we? We lie to avoid confrontation. So do kids. And here is one more reason why kids lie: When you're the last shiny object on the shelf, you've got to make stuff up because the other kids are talking about hockey practice and what they got to do with their moms and their dads. The kid in your class who doesn't have those stories because he has been in three different foster homes in three years? All he has is "We went to Disneyland last night," in an effort to get your connection. **From this day forward, every time you hear yourself say, "That kid is attention seeking or lying," try to replace that phrase with, "That kid is connection seeking," and see what happens.**

A Word on Diagnoses

Born With and Acquired

Part of what I learned from my team at the Children's Hospital was the importance of telling the story of kids. Often times, our focus is on their behavior and whether they were complying with the institutional expectations. The more difficulty they had, the more we worried that we weren't teaching them enough and so we tried to up our game. When the perception was that their behavior was willful or they were intentional in hurting us, it became so much more difficult to "be with" them and follow their need during their times of most significant distress.

The gold standard of diagnosing in our field means we often use the *Diagnostic and Statistical Manual of Mental Disorders*[40] now in its fifth revision. Diagnosing kids can often be helpful when identifying their most significant experiences. When it becomes unhelpful is when we label kids for the purposes of "coding" them or when we tell a "story" about them, based on what we know to be true about a particular diagnosis.

When it was my turn to tell the story of a kid to a group of people who believed the kid they were working with was attention seeking or intentionally manipulative, it became clear that my job was to get these well-meaning professionals back to a place of empathy. I did that by telling the kid's story. I found it most helpful to start talking about kids in terms of what they were "born with" and then what they had "acquired," often as a result of a mixture between their temperament and their life experiences.

In addition to learning disabilities,[41] some of the most common diagnoses often seen in schools are Oppositional Defiance Disorder (ODD), Conduct Disorder (CD), and Attention-Deficit/Hyperactivity Disorder (ADHD[42]). The first two, ODD (less serious behavioral and emotional dysregulation) and CD (more serious behavioral and emotional dysregulation), are used to describe kids who are defiant, who will not respect authority, and who make inappropriate or unacceptable, sometimes harmful, "choices." What is imperative to understand is that children are never "born with" either of those conditions. I think of these diagnoses as "acquired" based on their experiences. ODD and CD are descriptions of children who are dysregulated. Usually, these diagnoses are given not because there's something wrong with the child but because the people around that child (for a multitude of reasons) haven't been effective at assisting that kid in learning how to regulate emotion.

"Born with" diagnoses or conditions are things that have a neurological basis, diagnoses that tell us that kids have specific alterations in their brains or within the neurotransmitters of their brain that they have very little, if any, control over without intervention. Essentially, they came into this world "born with" these diagnoses. These include learning disabilities (there are three categories of disabilities: in Math, Reading, Writing, or a combination of these), clinical anxiety or depression, and more serious mental conditions like Obsessive Compulsive Disorder, Tourette's Syndrome, or schizophrenia. Standardized testing like cognitive or academic assessments also provide hard data on the capabilities of kids. Based on this assessment data and their "story," identifying what they were "born with" and what they "acquired" can be so helpful. Conversely, legitimate ADHD is a neurological condition that children are born with that can be treated with medication. I use the word "legitimate" because ADHD is one of the most frequently diagnosed disorders in children;[43] however, it is also misused to label children who are inattentive or hyperactive due to other experiences, including trauma.

When assessing kids, it became critical to me to know their story. I find it most helpful to complete a genogram with both the kids and the caregivers. A genogram is a pictorial representation of someone's family tree, with an emphasis on highlighting how everyone in a family is connected to one another and the relationships that exist between them. Knowing the facts of their family system, how they came into the world, and perceptions of relationships within a family system became the basis for conceptualizing or telling the story of a kid.

After assessing a child within the context of their family, I have found it most helpful to give their story back to the people who need to know it the most. In a school setting, this includes, but is not limited to, bus drivers, EAs, librarians, teachers, custodians, or administrative assistants—anyone who could be involved in helping this babe regulate. How I would describe this kid would always start with an explanation of what he was "born with" and then what he "acquired."

For example:

> *For this guy, we can be clear based on our assessment that he has a learning disability in math. That means he is smart, but that his academic math skills do not match what we would expect from his cognitive functioning. He was **born this way.** He is smart but will require modifications so that he can learn math.*
>
> *He also has had an extremely disruptive life, which has led to a host of diagnoses describing how his circumstances have affected him (**what he has acquired**). He trusts very few people, because he has been let down so many times. He is often irritable and does not respond well to authority. Subsequently, he was diagnosed with ODD.*

I would explain that this is what he has acquired as coping mechanisms based on how he's experienced the big people in his world. The goal in presenting children this way is so that those of us caring for them understand they have some things in their brain they cannot control.

We have to devise programs that support kids to be the best they can be. It's also important that we understand that the things children have acquired can be altered or made better by the way they are responded to by us and other professionals. This way of understanding kids has become the cornerstone of the **Carrington Connections Network for Educators** I developed for school divisions across the country (more on that in Chapter 5).

Is It Ever Too Late?

What happens if you have a kid who's had a horrific early start (like many kids in foster care have experienced)? What if they're in your classrooms as teenagers and have never had hands on the circle? Is it too late? Is it ever too late to help someone learn how to better regulate emotion?

I would not do what I do every single day—spend time away from my own babies, talking to anyone who will listen—if I believed for a second that it's ever, ever too late. In fact, in terms of neurodevelopment, adolescence is second only to the zero-to-two time frame. Opportunity to make significant inroads with adolescents becomes massively important as their teachers, mentors, and coaches spend time with them. I can develop a psychiatric condition in one interaction. Or, I can teach a kid they matter; I can teach them regulation, in just one interaction. And in case you're wondering, it's never too late for you (or that person you're raising/dating/living with/married to) to learn it either.

Remember, you cannot learn how to regulate emotion unless you are dysregulated first. What is cool (read: exhausting) about pre-teens and teenagers is there are tons of opportunities to teach regulation, because they're always flipping their lids. They provide us with endless opportunities to get their lids back on, don't they? Think about all the questions surrounding adolescents: What are you going to do with the rest of your life? You're in Grade 10. Your father and I would like to know your plan. Or, should you smoke? Should you drink? Are you going to try weed? Are you going to date? Have sex? Are you too fat? What is your gender identity? Are you going to eat a Tide Pod and put it on YouTube?

The stuff these (teenage) babies have on their shoulders is massive and they don't have a very well-developed prefrontal cortex to handle it (complete brain development occurs around age 25).[44] What becomes helpful for lid-flipping teens? It's hands on the circle co-navigating emotion and regulating with them that works. Kids cannot give away something they've never received. And co-regulating with teens often requires things like kindness, understanding, and a whole boatload of empathy and patience. The more they receive it, the greater access they have to these experiences when it comes time for them to give it away.

Emotional regulation becomes the most important factor when we talk attachment security in teens. Generally, if an adolescent has a secure relationship with just one adult, we see some remarkable differences in their choices compared to kids who struggle to find one regulated person to lean on regularly. The data is solid. With secure relationships, they are less likely to engage in violent behavior, there is less experimentation with substance abuse and risky sexual behavior, and they have greater capacity for managing frustration; kids who have secure relationships with adults tend to be popular with their peers yet less influenced by peer pressure. Here is what I love about this: When you have somebody in your world who can get your lid on, who can teach you how to regulate emotion, you will have access to making good choices. You also have access to what it means to be cool. You can sit around and talk about Snapchat and ask about the Blue Whale Challenge[45] and the show 13 Reasons Why.[46] When big decisions need to be made, like whether they should eat a Tide Pod, or drive home drunk from a party, they will have more access to the neuropathways that keep them regulated, and thus in touch with the stuff that results in better and safer decisions.

What's critical is for us to accept that all teenagers will flip their lids. That's their job. Even the ones who come from secure places will screw up—they're supposed to in order to learn how to navigate the world. What we know to be true is that they will just do it less frequently and perhaps less riskily if they have secure relationships with people in their world who have taught them (and continue to teach them) how to regulate emotion.

A Critical Note About Repair

Is it okay that kids lie? Or that they try to "manipulate" a situation? Of course not. Is it okay that kids yell, scream, swear, or are disrespectful to their elders? Of course not. It's not *if* you're going to teach that babe the importance of "making good choices" or "being respectful," it is *when*. You cannot teach a kid who is dysregulated. Getting the prefrontal cortex in place becomes the critical first step. Just how do you do that, you ask? I have a lot of ideas on that—all packaged nicely in Chapter 5.

I grappled long and hard about whether to make an entire chapter about repair. It's a simple concept that most people don't attend to nearly enough—but I think it's one of the most important things on the planet. Repair is about how to make a relationship better after you've had conflict (a rupture). Rupture and repair will happen in every single relationship that means anything to you. Dr. John M. Gottma says the capacity to repair in marital couples is the strongest predictor of couples who make it and couples who don't.[47] It makes sense then that we should focus a lot of time teaching our babies how to repair relationships, and how to apologize. But here's the thing—we're not very good at it either. And remember: We can't give away something we've never received.

Your most powerful tool—of all time—is timing. It's not **if** you're going to teach repair, it's **when**. We usually like to teach the most important lessons in our life when we're in the throes of despair. We know this because when others around us are in despair, particularly if we love them, we get in despair too. This means we flip our lids, we no longer have access to our best selves (prefrontal cortex), our ability to calm or soothe another is compromised, and our ability to make sense of hard things is weak. **Remember this: Whenever possible, follow a lead. Whenever necessary, take charge.**

It's in those "follow-the-lead" moments that repair and apology can happen for us too (we are the hands on the circle). We often want to follow every single apology with a "but." Seriously—just try to apologize to someone you love without using the word "but," and you'll see, it's damn near impossible. Repairing, apologizing, sinking into the emotion is often a critical component of the "collection" part of "collection before direction."[48] In fact, apologizing genuinely, not adding the word "but" afterward, is often one of the best gifts you can give your child (or anyone who matters to you).

The Bottom Line

There's a widespread need for common language, protocols, and role clarity not only in our province, but within our country, so that we can address the mental health concerns that are increasingly showing up in our classrooms. There's evidence that academic learning abilities become inaccessible to students who are emotionally unavailable.[49] And finally we're now beginning to accept that even if we have the most brilliant pedagogical lesson plans, fun white boards, bulletin boards that light up, or strict classrooms, kids cannot learn unless they're emotionally regulated first. That will be the most important lesson you will ever teach them.

CHAPTER THREE
Game Plan Highlight Reel

1. I have come to think of kids in three general, made-up-in-my-head categories: The regular lid flipper (where the majority of kids land), the Caillou, and the Flat Stanley. These babes all

have the exact same needs. How they pull for us to meet those needs makes all the difference.

2. Regular lid flippers (read: all kids) have one job and that is to flip their lids. All big people have one job: to help them get it back on. If you're a parent, your own personal child should be at their worst when they're with you—flipping their lid more often because they feel it is safest to do so. This allows our babes to stay regulated for longer when they're not with us.

3. Kids are not "attention seeking," they are "connection seeking," and they will "turn it up" in increasingly desperate ways when situations get dire, including doing things like lying, cheating, and stealing. It's our job to figure out *why* they're doing those things first. And then we teach.

4. It's not *if* we're going to address the inappropriate or unacceptable connection-seeking behaviors, it's when and how.

5. When reviewing a file for a kid who has a number of diagnoses, it's helpful to consider which labels they were "born with" and which ones they "acquired." It sometimes helps to put into perspective just what they (and we) have the control to influence.

So, game-changers, now that we know a little bit about just how influential you are, the next two chapters will equip you with a bit of background on two important things that often show up: **Trauma and grief**. Once we talk a little more about those two not-very-often-discussed-with-educators-but-so-friggin'-critical-to-know things, we can then talk about how you can help shape any kid (or any colleague) into the best they can be. If you'd like to know just how to do that, read on.

CHAPTER THREE

How I See Them

This chapter invites you to consider where kids these days might be coming from and what it might mean to face a world of false connection when you're trying to figure out if you matter. Here's a few discussion questions to get you started.

1. Talk about your understanding of my take on three kinds of kids: the regular lid flipper, Caillou, and Flat Stanley. Does this resonate? Did I miss any, in your experience?

2. What happens when you think of kids as connection seekers as opposed to attention seekers? How does this shift help you better help students?

3. When you think about the kids you teach or influence in your life who you are most worried about right now, what is the difference between the hand they were dealt (the things they were born with, like neurological conditions) versus things that they acquired via their experiences in this lifetime thus far. Share how, if at all, you think their experiences shape how they show up in the world.

AS IF IT WASN'T COMPLICATED ENOUGH

4

TRAUMA
COMPLICATES IT ALL

One of the most significant factors that contributes to lid flipping, but that we often overlook, is trauma. Trauma is more common than I wish it were. In fact, two-thirds of us have experienced at least one significant traumatic event in childhood, such as physical or sexual abuse, neglect, parental substance dependence, or mental illness.[50] Even though we experience these things when we're kids, they have the power to stay with us long into adulthood, both emotionally and physically. The goal in this chapter is to unpack what "trauma" means with a little bit of science and a lot of practical applications you can use with the people you teach, lead, and love.

When I started working with first responders and their families, what seems like a lifetime ago, my intrigue with trauma began. I spent as much time as these police officers and paramedics would let me on ride-alongs, where I was privy to their worst war stories. These women and men generally reserve those stories for only those who can "handle it," namely other first responders. They say the reason they don't talk about the hard stuff is confidentiality (which is generally true), and they don't like to share their pain with their loved ones because they don't want their loved ones to share in the horrors. And a third reason, which I think is significant, is they don't talk about it so they don't have to relive what they would rather forget.

Talking through trauma, making sense of hard things, isn't generally enjoyable. This is particularly true if the trauma is heartbreaking. But talking through it is necessary. These words from Bessel van der Kolk summarize it so well:

> *Traumatized people chronically feel unsafe inside their bodies: The past is alive in the form of gnawing interior discomfort. Their bodies are constantly bombarded by visceral warning signs, and, in an attempt to control these processes, they often become expert at ignoring their gut feelings and in numbing awareness of what is played out inside. They learn to hide from their selves.*[51]

I am continually shocked at how much we ask police officers to go through every day, and how little they talk about what they see. This would become, years later, the focus of my doctoral dissertation: The Effect of Trauma on Police Marriages (2006) from the University of Regina. During my research and later, in my clinical residency, I was amazed how little we knew about kids and trauma. This brings us here today and is why we need to talk about this with those of you who care for our babies every day. I can't think of anyone more important to share this with than those of you charged with influencing our future generations. I hope, sweet educators, you will find this chapter a helpful reference.

Trauma: A Big Word That is More Common Than I Wish It Were

Everyone has a story that might break your heart. And although words like "trauma-informed" and "trauma-sensitive" have become mainstream in education, there has yet to be a national standard adopted across the USA or Canada. In a recent review of the national and international literature, University of British Columbia researchers Record-Lemon and Buchanan[52] reported that there's a scarcity of empirical knowledge regarding effective trauma-informed practices (TIPs)[53] with children in Canadian schools. This has been highlighted specifically within the last two years, as more than 20,000 of the Syrian refugees who have settled in Canada are under the age of 18. A number of these children have significant trauma histories (coming from a war-torn country) often with language barriers that add to the difficulty in programming, educating, and supporting.

In Canada, there are a select few programs available that help to create an understanding of what trauma looks like in the classroom and how best to respond to students. One of note includes initiatives by Safer Schools Together.[54] In addition, the North American Center for Threat Assessment and Trauma Response[55] has developed a widely adopted protocol (the Violence Threat Risk Assessment protocol) that is used to assess and respond to students who are identified as threats, including how to respond to a crisis within a community.[56] There is, however, very little focus on how we care for the educators who will have to hold these stories of trauma in increasing numbers.

We will spend time in this darker chapter talking about the things you must know as an educator, not to make it harder or more heartbreaking, but to shed some light and to arm you with resources to better understand and respond to the stories and the kids involved.

What Does It Mean to Be Trauma-Informed?

Being "trauma informed" has become a particularly important standard of practice these days for many service providers. Dr. Susan E. Craig, in *Trauma-Sensitive Schools: Learning Communities Transforming Children's Lives, K—5*,[57] highlights the importance of understanding how trauma works in kids, and the necessity to have informed policy and practices that will make responses to these babes helpful, not harmful. Dr. Patricia A. Jennings wrote *The Trauma-Sensitive Classroom*,[58] which brilliantly emphasizes the need to "draw on the power of the story" while ensuring that we are looking after educators first. Further, an initiative by the Beyond Consequences Institute[59] developed a valuable administrator's guide titled *The Trauma-Informed School: A Step-by-Step Implementation Guide for Administrators and School Personnel*,[60] where they outline a standard of practice.

Defining what constitutes a "trauma" can be difficult. Essentially, no experience is "traumatic" unless it is an experience encoded with terror. That experience, coupled with terror, results in a traumatic experience.[61] Depending on each individual's experience, most anything can be coupled with terror. Thus, a psychological injury occurs. And much like a physical injury, it must receive an intervention in order to heal properly.

Children with a significant history of trauma do not benefit from a traditional behavioral approach where we reward the good behavior and punish the bad stuff. What we tend to be punishing (with suspensions and expulsions), is actually emotional dysregulation. We punish in the hopes that when we take enough stuff away from these "bad kids," they will learn how to be kind and "make good choices." This misguided intention to help these kids "make good choices" often results in us big people responding in ways that can be even more harmful. We're punishing them for the lack of skill they don't yet have, or for a psychological injury that has yet to be healed.

All of that said (and please review the resources above for more details of this amazing work), what is necessary in becoming trauma-informed is to be clear on the (extensive) research and understand what's been compiled about how trauma affects development. There's a substantial amount of information out there; however, we have yet to integrate it into our current teaching practices to the extent that's not only critical, but necessary. What we know to be true is that disruptions in initial attachment relationships interfere with the development of representational thought (this is the underpinning of language, empathy, memory, executive functioning, and attention), which are all of the things necessary for children to learn in a classroom and to "make good choices" in relationships on the playground. The data on the effects of trauma aren't nearly as understood or mainstream as I wish. Highlighting just how critical it is to create a better understanding of trauma in our communities and in our classrooms, let me take you through a very basic journey of trauma. I am going to start with the most profound research on trauma. If you're not yet familiar with the Adverse Childhood Experience (ACE) study, I need to tell you, this work is the most informative in the world of trauma I know of to date.[62] Absorbing this, in my opinion, is crucial for any of us who want to consider ourselves "trauma-informed."

Adverse Childhood Experiences

The lead on the ACE research, Dr. Vincent J. Felitti,[63] stumbled on this powerful data following what was supposed to be research about weight loss. He observed many of the unsuccessful weight loss participants shared a common experience: They had all experienced sexual abuse as a child.

If I had my way, the Adverse Childhood Experiences study would become an important component of all assessments of kids and be used as the foundation in telling their story. Trauma history is so important to consider when programming in the classroom because the behavior we see on the outside is reflective of their brains working differently (as a result of trauma) on the inside, and not willful acts of defiance.

Adverse Childhood Experiences

Category of Abuse:

1. Physical abuse
2. Emotional abuse
3. Sexual abuse

Category of Neglect:

4. Physical neglect
5. Emotional neglect

Category of Household Dysfunction:

6. Growing up with someone in your home who suffers from a mental illness
7. Growing up with someone in your home who experiences substance abuse
8. Having an incarcerated relative
9. Witnessing the mother being treated violently
10. Divorced parents

Curious and armed with funding, the team of Dube, Anda, Felitti, Chapman, Williamson, and Giles gathered an unprecedentedly large sample of over 17,000 adult participants and asked them questions about childhood experiences and their current level of functioning.[64] In this groundbreaking research, they identified the 10 strongest predictors of adult adversity and summarized them into three categories: abuse, neglect, and household dysfunction. Within these three categories, there are 10 things that, if you have experienced them before the age of 18, will become cumulatively predictive of struggles in adulthood (how "struggle" is defined or experienced in adults will vary). The assessment method is simple: You get a point for each of the 10 that you have experienced before the age of 18. Points, in this case, aren't something you want.

The ACE researchers identified that four or more points before age 18 means you are:

- 3x more likely to be a smoker
- 6x more likely to have had an unplanned teen pregnancy
- 7x more likely to have been involved in violence in the last year
- 11x more likely to have used heroin/crack or been incarcerated
- 18x more likely to attempt suicide

When I review this research, people wonder why other things did not make the list, such as death of a parent or car accidents. Those experiences can be traumatizing, of course, but what's so interesting about this research is it was statistically proven that these ten carry the most predictive power. So, although it might not make sense, it's the strongest ten that will predict later (dys)functioning in adulthood.

Anyone can calculate their ACE score. As noted above, if you answer yes to any of those experiences, you get a point. What is compelling, and also heartbreaking, is having just **four** points appears to be the tipping point. Any of us who experiences four or more, without intervention, will struggle more often in adulthood with relationship issues, substance issues, and physical ailments than people who don't experience as many ACEs. How I make sense of this is that **the more experiences of disconnect you have in childhood, the more you will numb in adulthood**. The result is significant emotional dysfunction, as well as increased physical illness and/or disease. Those numbers are staggering and critical for those who care for our babies every day. Dr. Bessel van der Kolk, author of *The Body Keeps the Score* (my trauma-related bible)[65] put forth this profound statement, following a review of the ACE research:

> *As the ACE study has shown, child abuse and neglect is the single most preventable cause of mental illness, the single most common cause of drug and alcohol abuse, and a significant contributor to leading causes of death such as diabetes, heart disease, cancer, stroke, and suicide.*

Trauma and the Brain

Post-Traumatic Stress Disorder

Post-Traumatic Stress Disorder (PTSD) is a focus in the mental health world, most often discussed when referencing war veterans or first responders. Although many times children don't get the "label" of PTSD, I still think it's helpful to understand the diagnosis that explains what it looks like when our difficult experiences start to interfere with our functioning. PTSD is not age-specific; kids of any age can experience trauma that may result in post-trauma symptoms and potentially PTSD. Children and teens who go through the most severe trauma tend to have the highest levels of PTSD symptoms. We all have difficult experiences, every day. The majority of us can make sense of these things, often with the help of others, and we move on, but when we do not have someone to help us through these processes (such as might be the case for these kids), we start to experience symptoms that can look like PTSD.

PTSD is technically defined as a psychiatric disorder that can occur in people who have experienced or witnessed a traumatic event.[66] In general, people with PTSD continue to have intense, disturbing thoughts and feelings related to their experience(s) that can last long after the traumatic event(s) has ended. Essentially, they continue to live as though they're still in the middle of the event and their body responds accordingly. They may relive the event through flashbacks or nightmares; they may feel sadness, fear, or anger; and they may feel detached or estranged from other people. With kids, sometimes spontaneous and intrusive memories may not necessarily appear distressing and may be expressed as play re-enactment.

The four categories of PTSD symptoms are: intrusive thoughts (unwanted memories); mood alterations (shame, blame, persistent negativity); hypervigilance (exaggerated startle response); and avoidance (of all sensory and emotional trauma-related material). These cause confusion for partners and families of survivors, who don't understand how people they formerly knew and loved suddenly become so out of control in their own minds and bodies.

People of all ages with PTSD may avoid situations or people who remind them of the traumatic event, and they may have strong negative reactions to something as ordinary as a loud noise or an accidental touch. I want to be very clear about one thing: **PTSD is NOT a mental illness; it is a psychological injury**. And just like a physical injury, treating it early and with an effective intervention will result in healing.

PTSD is an elusive compilation of symptoms that has been designed to address what we know to be true: If we do not respond to people who have experienced life-threatening or extremely fearful situations, their subsequent functioning will be affected. In my work over the years with police officers and other first responders, I have had my heart broken a time or two as I watch grown humans (mostly men), whose desire it once was to make this world a better place, be trapped behind walls and walls of trauma. They can't cry anymore. They can't feel joy anymore. They are just "stuck" in a place that has become safer than feeling. They're numb. And when feelings start to creep in (as they inevitably will), these heroes find ways to stay externally numb—like with sex, drugs, food, or alcohol.

Throughout the brain, several chemical and biological imbalances can present after trauma. Specific physical changes in the brain occur that can be observed and measured in CAT scans or MRIs, further supporting that trauma responses are not just an inability to "get over it." More specifically, researchers have focused on the amygdala, an almond-shaped mass located deep in the brain responsible for survival-related threat identification, plus tagging memories with emotion.

With trauma, the amygdala can get caught up in a highly alert and activated loop during which it looks for and perceives threat everywhere. Secondly, researchers have observed significant changes in the hippocampus (another component in the limbic system), such as an increase in the stress hormones that destroy healthy cells, which leaves it less effective in making synaptic connections necessary for solidifying memories. This interruption keeps both the body and mind stimulated in reactive mode as neither element receives the message that the threat is no longer imminent. Finally, the constant elevation of stress hormones (such as cortisol) interfere with the body's ability to regulate itself, thus flipping the lid way more often than in those who have had fewer traumatic experiences. And the sympathetic nervous system (of which the amygdala is a part) remains highly activated, leading to fatigue of the body and many of its systems. For further reading, some of my favorites who helped me make sense of it all are Nadine Burke Harris, Michele Rosenthal, Bruce Perry, and Bessel van der Kolk, all phenomenal.

Before we go any further, I want to be clear that while changes to the brain can seem, on the surface, disastrous and representative of permanent damage, the truth is that all of these alterations can be reversed. The amygdala can learn to relax, the hippocampus can resume proper memory consolidation, and the nervous system can get back to its easy flow between reactive and settling-down ways. I wouldn't do what I do every day if I didn't believe that to be true (and there's significant evidence to support what I believe[67]). We will talk about how you can assist in that process in a little bit.

But before we do, I want to focus in on two significant issues that often arise in our schools these days, with little direction or support provided for teachers. First, a chapter on trauma would be remiss, in my opinion, if we did not discuss one of the most fearful issues facing classrooms these days: school shootings and how they fit in to this world of being trauma-informed. Secondly, we need to discuss experiences with trauma that kids in state/foster care face, which is an increasingly common experience among some children in our country.

School Shooters Always Have a Trauma History

I think these students are, without exception, connected to trauma histories. I want to be very clear that having a trauma history does not mean you grow up to be a school shooter. Although school shootings receive significant attention in the media, they remain rare, even in the United States. These tragedies, however, are happening more frequently in the USA—there were three school shootings from 1966 to 1975 and that number increased to at least 89 incidents of gunfire on school grounds in 2018 alone (see EveryTown for Gun Safety for a review[68]). According to EveryTown, there have been 290 incidents since 2013. These incidents range from mass shootings to accidental discharges of firearms, after-hours fights between adults in a school parking lot to suicides. This increase leaves many understandably concerned that similar numbers are "imminent" in Canada.

The American psychologist Dr. Peter Langman, is considered one of the foremost experts in the area of school shootings in the USA.[69] He notes that school shooters typically fall under one of three psychological categories. The first, he says, is the "psychopathic personality." The second is the "psychotic school shooter," who is not fully grounded in reality. And the third category, he suggests, is the "traumatized school shooter." He describes these kids as being from horrendous family backgrounds who have experienced multiple types of abuse, chronic stress, and trauma. It occurs to me, however, that even the first two categories that Langman identifies can still involve students with a trauma history. Furthermore, children who develop a "psychopathic personality" are not born that way.[70] Personality disorders, by definition, develop as coping mechanisms in response to traumatizing relationships around them. What I believe to be true is that no infant is born wanting to shoot up a school.

A "psychotic school shooter" would be considered someone with a mental illness who is experiencing acute psychotic reactions and who develops hallucinations and delusions. As a psychologist, I can tell you that these children are very easy to identify, as their functioning is significantly affected. These rare but confusing and fear-inducing symptoms also result in traumatic experiences for the child. Thus, although school shooters might have different backgrounds and experiences, there has yet to be a school shooter who, at least in retrospect, acted in a manner that surprised us. We know who the kids we're most worried about are. What we need to be more focused on, though, is how to create a village around these kids so they don't have to turn it up (i.e., shoot up a school) to get their needs met.

As I was writing this chapter, another school shooting in the United States of America occurred in Parkland, Florida. The questions following this "most massive school shooting in history" had many demanding changes to gun laws and school policies. And then another happened in Santa Fe, Texas, as I was editing this chapter. And, sadly, I am going to guess that before this book is published, another one (or more) will have happened. In the aftermath of a tragedy, we are compelled to put our anger and our rage somewhere. We demand reform. We demand change. We want to fix what's broken, fueled by the fear that it might happen to us. Mostly we demand that someone take control and we focus on the behavior. Calls to action are everywhere—our first response is fight or flight. How do we protect and take care of our most precious resource? The immediate response after Columbine was a "zero-tolerance policy." This meant that we expelled anyone who even talked about guns, thereby pushing out the very kids who need connection the most. Gun control, not surprisingly, remained the focus to "fight back" with something bigger (despite the fact that it still doesn't work to change things). According to data from the National Conference of State Legislatures, since the Parkland shooting, at least 14 states have introduced measures that would enable educators to carry firearms on the job (in their schools!); however, as I was writing this chapter, only one of these measures has been voted into law, in Florida.

The answer, in my humble opinion, is not only about gun control. Here it comes again—so wait for it. Without a doubt, it comes down to connection. And the other thing no one is talking about: Whether or not **our educators** are okay. It's *not* resources and support for the kids, but for the people who hold them. Why aren't school shootings more common in Canada? I truly believe it's very much connected to the way we treat our educators. Now, let me say that there is so much about gun control that I cannot even begin to debate or understand, all of which is beyond the scope of this book. My focus here is about connection and without it, all the gun-control interventions will not change things.

Our kids are now standing up to advocate for change by talking about guns (and gun companies that fund politicians), and about mental illness and support, because they believe that the big people are not listening. We are not listening to them when they shoot us, and we are still not listening when they calmly take over the world. Instead our leaders scrap it out with threats and revocation of tariffs because they are afraid of gun control. What the big people are missing is that school shootings are not only about guns. We have to acknowledge that school shootings are also about missed connections. We have continually missed their cues (for connection), we have continually punished their "bad behavior" by expelling or alienating them, and they just keep getting louder. You can only catch a cue if, as a big person (educator or parent), you're supported, appreciated, and filled up enough to pay attention.

There is not a single school shooter who was a surprise to us, in retrospect. Not one who we didn't have concerns about before he shot up the school (and invariably it's primarily men who participate in gun violence). These babes had been "turning it up" and "seeking bottom hands" for months or years before they did the shooting. What they did is unimaginable. How they got there, however, is remarkably predictable and something we simply don't talk about enough. Especially when we're scared. So, take a deep breath, and let's talk about it here.

Kids in Care in Canada

In 2013, there were an estimated 62,428 children in out-of-home state-run care across Canada.[71] Because child welfare services fall under the jurisdiction of provincial and territorial authorities, each province has different legislation pertaining to child protection interventions, making it difficult to compare rates of children apprehended. That being said, researchers tell us the Canadian province Manitoba has the highest rate of kids in care.[72]

According to the 2016 Canadian Census of Population, Indigenous children represent only 7.7% of the total population aged 0 to 14 in Canada. They account, however, for over half (52.2%) of children in foster care.[73] There is a colonial history of oppression, abuse, neglect, and trauma against First Nations people in Canada. The 60s Scoop and the Indian Residential School system are horrific wounds that run very deep leading to intergenerational trauma.[74] If we consider the science of ACE research, it stands to reason that multiple generations of First Nations people have been traumatized with very few positive interventions (not just money) and continue to struggle to develop emotional regulation skills today. Generation after generation of abuse, neglect, and trauma makes it difficult to do better. **You can't give away something you have never received.**

The rationale for putting kids in care has been to provide foster care for those who need safety from biological parents who are unable to care for their children for various reasons. What we continue to largely fail at, however, is to concurrently provide corrective experiences for their parents or grandparents. There's a long and detailed history of our broken system that is plagued with funding cuts and lack of support for fostering, adoptive, and biological families. Once again, we're failing to look after the most important resource: those holding the children. The kids will not have a corrective experience if they're placed in homes where those holding them feel a lack of support, are over-extended, or traumatized as well. Children in care often return to their biological families once they age out of the system, and the lack of intervention with those biological families means those children will return to a system that continues to be unhealthy. Recently in Alberta, a Ministerial Panel was convened to make recommendations on how to improve the child intervention system. Their final report, *Walking as one: Ministerial Panel on Child Intervention's final recommendations to the Minister of Children's Services*, includes 26 recommendations.[75]

Similarly, in the United States in 2016 there were 437,465 kids in foster care.[76] They too report underfunded and under-resourced children and family services. The irony doesn't escape me that the most vulnerable children often have overworked and overwhelmed people trying to help them navigate during the most difficult experiences of their lives. These agencies and systems consistently lack sustainable funding to enrich and support everyone involved. As you've heard me say before, we're wired to survive hard things; but we will not survive them well, if at all, if we're not connected with at least one regulating other person who can help us make sense of it.

Knowing a kid's story becomes particularly important if they are or have been in foster care. In collaboration with a number of school divisions in Canada, we have finally begun to develop a model that makes the story the primary focus. See Chapter 7 for a review of the **Carrington Connection Network for Educators** to see if it might serve as a road map for your school division or district (more on that in a bit).

Armor Up

Our First Response to Trauma

In the absence of having a story and support that allows us to regulate, we respond in a primal manner: We armor up and close off from others. That's the natural response to pain, even emotional pain. Think about what happens to your body when you're about to fall off your bike. Or when you're going in for a rough landing on an airplane. Or going into labor. You brace for it. You tense up and get ready for it. Although this is sometimes initially helpful, what helps most is to lean into the pain and on to other people who can help you regulate through it.

One form of armor we often use in our best efforts to understand kids is to label them. It becomes so difficult to truly label "trauma" correctly and we often don't get it right. Dr. van der Kolk summarized this beautifully when he said:

> *Eighty-two percent of the traumatized children seen in the National Child Traumatic Stress Network do not meet diagnostic criteria for PTSD. Because they often are shut down, suspicious, or aggressive they now receive pseudoscientific diagnoses such as "oppositional defiant disorder," meaning "This kid hates my guts," or "disruptive mood dysregulation disorder," meaning he has temper tantrums. These kids accumulate numerous diagnoses over time. Before they reach their twenties, many patients have been given four, five, six, or more of these impressive but meaningless labels. If they receive*

*treatment at all, they get whatever is being promulgated
as the method of management du jour: Medications,
behavioral modification, or exposure therapy. These
rarely work and often cause more damage.*

The understandable response to trauma for adult or kid victims is
to protect oneself by shutting down or getting mad. When you have
seen, heard, felt, and smelled horrible things over and over again,
it becomes more comfortable to stay behind our walls and trust no
one. And for those trying to assist the people who have experienced
trauma, labeling and trying to "fix it" is often something we get
caught up in easily. Trauma itself, however, doesn't cause damage.
The damage occurs when the person experiencing the trauma feels
helpless in the face of it, encodes the experience with terror, and
copes by shutting down. Often, these babies have few relationships
that have been supportive enough to hold their hurts and teach
them how to stay connected through the hard stuff. So, their go-to
in times of distress remains fight, flight, or freeze. If we're to change
that, we need to stay connected to them. We can't accomplish that
when we simply reward the good stuff and punish the bad stuff. We
miss their story and would likely respond so differently if we asked
why they're acting the way they are. In our well-intentioned desire
to teach good behavior, we miss their story. We miss the fear. We
miss the sadness. We just see the mad. And remember, **mad is just
sad's bodyguard**. But you have to get through mad before you can
get to sad.

So, Now What?

If we want to consider long and lasting change, we must come back
to the fundamentals. We can only assist kids if we're okay. The
focus, I think, needs to be less on the children and more on the
people who hold them, educate them, and assist them. We need to

not only identify with it, but to respond to these children from a place of connection.

There are several successful models in the United States, where some schools have integrated trauma-informed policies and practices into classrooms and playgrounds.[77] Researchers report that these schools experience a 90 percent drop in suspensions after one year implementing trauma-informed practices. After three years, the schools no longer expel students and some no longer even have the need for in-school suspensions. The grades, test scores, and graduation rates increased, and the students who benefited most were those with the highest ACE scores. By the end of 2017, several hundred schools across the USA were integrating trauma-informed and resilience-building practices based on ACE science; however, there is still no national standard.

In Canada, although we're becoming more familiar with ACE and how it affects our students, we too don't have a national standard of practice. We need to do better. I have some ideas on how to create a national standard of practice (more on that in Chapter 7!). For now, I have come up with a few things I hope will be helpful to keep in mind if (and likely when) you have a kid who has a trauma history and who needs you to be the regulating other. These babes will not make it easy. You will need to remember this and be reminded of it again and again when things get tough.

Taking Down the Armor

Here are some things to consider if you have a babe with a trauma history in your classroom. Dr. Peter A. Levine, a trauma expert, shares: "Trauma is not what happens to us, but what we hold inside in the absence of an empathic witness."[78] Wow, right?! Read that sentence again. The most critical thing I want you to remember, above all else, is that anyone who has experienced trauma, either acute or chronic, just needs a space to put it. These kids and families need a "village" to help remind them that they are safe and that they matter. Then, and only then, can they be taught literacy and numeracy.

Often times, our schools become a place of refuge or a place people gather to make sense of hard things, particularly in our rural communities. Often when a tragedy or a critical incident takes place (e.g., car accidents, forest fires), educators become the first professionals who are sought out to regulate others. If you're involved with students within the first few hours or even days following a traumatic incident, you will see what we all universally experience—that is, shaking, nausea, increased blood pressure, "depersonalization" or zoning out, sweating, or shivering. Here are a few things to consider that may be most beneficial when (not if) you will be called upon to help kids who have just been through a trauma and who need to regulate and feel safe again. Here is a guide to support you in that work.

Immediately Following a Trauma

1. Create Safety

- Slow down any external noise and reassure them they're safe now. It might feel weird, in some contexts, to say, "You are safe now," but it's often a very clear message to the nervous system that is needed. And repeat it.
- Set up a predictable place where students are aware of what is about to happen. Explaining a "plan" and its concrete steps is helpful. For example, "We have called your parents, Principal Jones is going to meet them at the door, while we stay here with you. We have juice and cookies here. We will sit with you until we know there's someone safe who you can go home with."

2. Regulate the Nervous System

- There are a number of things that serve to ground us when we're feeling distressed. We will talk more about these in Chapter 6 but consider having something to drink—even water—available. If you're able, have a snack available. This is ideal because you cannot chew and swallow with a flipped lid; however, it can be difficult for anyone to eat when in the state of immediate crisis or shock.
- Get eye contact if you can, even if it means saying things like, "Look at me." If physical touch is something that is warranted, this is often helpful to get people back into the moment. It can also help to guide them to slow down their breathing or bring them back into their bodies (e.g., wiggle your toes in your shoes, feel your shirt on your back).

3. Listen, Don't Fix

- I cannot stress this enough—there's nothing you can say immediately following a significant crisis that is going to fix it, so don't try. Focus instead on what you notice around you: "I see your heart is broken. I can see it's even hard to breathe." Or, use these two phrases that always save my bacon: "Tell me more," and, if appropriate, "What happened next?" This keeps people talking and avoids you from falling into the trap of "fixing" or offering solutions that often start with the words "at least." If you hear yourself saying "at least," stop in your tracks, because although your intention is noble, right now a "fix" will not be helpful.

4. Leave Them with a Plan

- Once you have regulated the best you can, end with a plan. For example, "Your parents are going to take you home now. They've got you. I will check in with you tomorrow morning at 9:00 a.m.." Or, "The school will be open again tomorrow at noon, and we would love to see you back here to answer any questions that might come up overnight as we make sense of these things."

Preparing for and Responding to Kids with Chronic Trauma

There are a few things I would like you to consider for kids who have experienced ACEs, when you know a student has experienced significant trauma and is now on your bus route or coming into your classroom. I want you to remember grace. Trauma inevitably flips lids faster, which means these babes (and often their parents) are not operating from a calm and regulated space. You can imagine if you've been in a state of "fight or flight" for months or even years, you may be irritable, suspicious, or hyper-vigilant. Kids with a chronic trauma history experience sleep disturbance, nightmares, somatization (physical aches and pains), elevated cortisol levels (the stress hormone), and hyper-arousal. Depending on how the big people in their world have responded to their experiences, an ACE score alone will not predict how children or their families will recover, but here are a few things to keep in mind and potentially review with the "village" who will hold them.

Oh—speaking of the "village," one thing that has struck me as troublesome is that the toughest babes are often treated or educated in isolation. The thing is, breaking down the armor and teaching emotional regulation is tough, tough work. Even the most seasoned veterans will get worn down, beat themselves up for not "getting through," become exhausted and overwhelmed. These babes require a village of people who collectively understand their story and can take over the regulating process, especially when times get tough. I have thought long and hard about how to best create "villages" in education systems. With the help of some very smart educators, I share what we have learned in detail in Chapter 7. For now, here's a short reference list I hope will be helpful for you and the village educating a kid who has a long-standing story of trauma.

Immediately Following a Trauma for Kids with Chronic Trauma

1. **Create Safety**
   - This is a repeat of the first step in what to do following an immediate trauma; however, this is more about preparing the environment. When first meeting a student, I want you to choose one or two people on staff who will work to become their "person." It's who will meet them at the door every morning if possible, and who they can lean on when things get tough. I have heard often that children should not get too attached to one person, so there is a tendency to change their person often. This is a harmful practice. Creating a safe and secure relationship with one person at a time is most effective with kids who have a trauma history. In fact, it's crucial.
   - I appreciate the challenge you have when students arrive in your schools or on your buses and you have virtually no background information on them. Whenever possible, it's so helpful if you know something about their story, like a sport they play or a video game they like. This knowledge can give you a powerful opener.

2. **Build a Connected Relationship**
   - Within the first day, and often longer, academics should be the least of your worries. You may want to introduce them to the classroom but getting to know them before you ever start teaching them is imperative. I cannot stress this enough. Day one and maybe week one, month one, or even year one should be about learning who they are. If resources are available, get them to tell, or draw, or write about who they are and what they like, and get at least one person "in" and able to influence in the days and weeks ahead. Finding something these kids love will be your only goal.

- Then, learning all about their thing will be the direct path to creating a sense of safety for them. For example, if a student who has been in care for the past five years starts at your school, after being in three different spots in the past two years, I want you to know what the one thing is that he's crazy about. Maybe it is Pokémon, Fortnight, or Miley Cyrus (don't judge me—I'm a child of the 90s). Whatever it is, that needs to be all you learn about for at least the first day, maybe the first week of school. Proceed slowly, and with all due respect. Doing so will give you a remarkable amount of power to "push" for requests when you need these kids to start engaging in the academics. Building a relationship with them is not the endgame. There will come a time to teach. But connection must come first.

3. Regulate the Nervous System and then Teach

We will discuss how to capture a kid's heart in Chapter 6; however, it's important to regulate to get that lid back on as quick and as often as you can. Consider things like:

- Start each day the same way: Have the same person or two meet the kid's eyes every day. It's always helpful if the kid likes this person and, more importantly, the person likes this kid. Knowing what to expect is calming.
- Know that your student will function best if they're able to drink and eat at any given time even while in the classroom. Eating is a clue that their lid is on (because you cannot swallow with a flipped lid—more on that in Chapter 6).
- See the five keys to (re)connecting coming up in the next chapter. These will be absolutely critical, as babes with a trauma history can sometimes have difficulty staying present.
- I want you to remember that their story will come up for reasons we (and they) may never understand and so it's often

not helpful to determine an exhaustive list of "triggers." You are not going to get them all. What becomes critical is having a plan when they do become dysregulated (which will likely happen often).

4. Plan For the Worst

If you know your student has a history of acting out, aggression, or verbal displays of emotion, it will be important to know what's going to happen when that goes down. And remember, when it does, know that is exactly what we want. Walking through this with your most broken students will be the most important thing you ever teach them.

5. Focus on Resiliency and Regulation Skills

- Whenever possible, take the opportunity to put these babes in positions where they will get to practice staying regulated. Sometimes we steer clear of assigning tasks to the lid flippers for fear that they will not handle it. But it's the only way they will learn it. Often pairing them with another student and walking them through social skills when problems arise will be way more effective than having them complete a social skills group assignment.

6. Fostering Post-Trauma Growth

- It is sometimes difficult to see the forest for the trees, especially with babes who we find ourselves in the trenches with every day. These kids, and the staff holding them, will benefit from frequent reviews of progress, no matter how small. I often say to kids, even a few weeks in, "Remember in your first week, you were not even able to enter the classroom? Today you did work for two whole periods!" Even more important is highlighting progress with staff to keep them in the game too. Things as small as observing regulated interactions or smiles between a dysregulated student and a particular staff member are often things we miss when we are "waiting for the shoe to drop."

The Bottom Line

So, that's a wrap on trauma. To be honest, I have tried to end this chapter about 20 times, and then I keep remembering another thing I want you to know. In the end, I want you to remember that trauma complicates it all. Now you know about the ACE, it will give you a sense of what "trauma" really means. And being "trauma-informed" means that you now know many experiences will alter the way kids respond to you. This will require grace, and acknowledging that they cannot learn if we do not address their stories first. And just in case you're thinking of all the kids who you might have "missed it" with, remember these words (they always afford me grace):

"Do the best you can until you know better. Then when you know better, do better."

—Maya Angelou

I hope the information here will help you navigate even just a bit better with those toughest babes. And there are a ton of resources in the Notes and References section of the book where you can find some of the "big shooters" in this world of trauma.

CHAPTER FOUR

Game Plan Highlight Reel

1. Traumatic experiences are common. In fact, rarely (never) will we get through this life without experiencing something that we require another human to help us make sense of.

2. Findings of the Adverse Childhood Experiences (ACE) Study have become the most powerful evidence that if certain experiences (ten to be exact) occur in childhood, there is indisputable evidence to suggest that the child will struggle both physically and emotionally as an adult if no intervention is provided.

3. Being trauma-informed in a school system means educating all staff in what trauma means and the subsequent effects on behavior and learning these experiences can have. Developing policy and procedures from this perspective requires a significant shift from a behavioral model of teaching and discipline practices to a relationship-based philosophy.

4. PTSD is not a mental illness; it is a psychological injury. Just like a physical injury, treating trauma early and with the most informed approach will result in the most efficient and effective healing. In this chapter, you'll find a playbook as a reference when and if those you teach, lead, and love experience trauma. I hope this will help to support you.

5. In my opinion, the answers to addressing the fear of and the actual school shootings in North America has very little to do with gun control and arming teachers and way more to do about how we treat and care for our educators.

Before we step into my humble offering of the "answers to it all" part of the book, I want to take one hot minute (a small chapter) on the big topic of grief. It's necessary. It will not be a lot of fun because grief rarely is. But I've learned that braving the waves of grief means trusting that the hard parts will not last forever. They will come and go. You will have a student, or a colleague, who will have to brave the waves. And you will too. For my insights about grief, read on, dear ones.

CHAPTER FOUR

Trauma Complicates It All

My biggest insights around understanding trauma and its implications in relationships came most pointedly when I started to understand trauma as a psychological injury, rather than a mental illness. Use that as your springboard as you launch into some discussion.

1. What is your understanding of what it means to be "trauma-informed" or "trauma-sensitive"? How do you think having an understanding of trauma might affect your practice or how you show up with babies in your classrooms or your communities (your kids' friends, the ones you coach, the ones you see at the hockey rink)?

2. The Adverse Childhood Experiences Study is one of the most profound research undertakings in the world of trauma. Discuss the ten ACEs identified by Felitti and colleagues and what it might take to "erase an ACE.

3. What are some of your biggest takeaways when thinking about interacting with children who have a history of trauma? If you could have the people in your world understand just one thing about trauma, what might that be?

THE GREAT
EQUALIZER

5

GRIEF

Grief is the great equalizer. If you're old enough to love, you're old enough to grieve. But no one really likes to talk about grief. At first, I thought it safer to hide these words in the chapter on trauma—a sexier version of grief. I settled on the fact, however, that not everyone experiences trauma, but everyone, at some point, will experience grief. We need to talk about it in a slightly different way. So, here we are, in a lonely little chapter where grief takes center stage.

Despite the fact that you will not get off this planet without experiencing grief in some form, at some time, most of us continue to struggle with helping people through grief. In fact, everyone you cross paths with today will have a story of grief, loss, and/or death. These three are the great equalizers. The process of grief, loss, and death are universal, but we rarely talk about how grief and loss might show up in the classroom. As an educator, it's inevitable that you will provide care for a grieving child during your teaching career. In fact, one in 20 children will lose a parent by the age of 15, and almost all children experience the death of a close family member or friend by the time they finish high school.[79] Yet, only seven percent of teachers say they have any bereavement training. Loss has major implications for learning, as grief can mean academic, behavioral, and social issues. We need to do better.

What Do We Know About Grief?

In 1969, Dr. Elisabeth Kübler-Ross[80] proposed that the five stages of grief occurred in a linear fashion. Since that highly-referenced original work, others, including Kübler-Ross herself, have clarified that grief is anything but a linear process. What we know today is there are no "stages" of grief, but rather there are just emotions. Big, huge, fat, scary emotions that often come in waves. When we're at the crest of a wave, we fear, and in fact are often convinced, it will never end and we will be stuck in the hell of pain and loss forever. When the wave ebbs, we often believe everything is fine and grieving is done.

The truth of the matter is aptly stated by the infamous (to me anyway) Dr. Brené Brown:[81]

> *Rarely can a response make something better. What makes something better is connection.*

If you've heard me speak, you know this quote resonates within my soul and I repeat it as often as I can. We're so inclined to "fix" hurt, to relieve someone's emotional pain, to calm dysregulated emotions, particularly when they're present in someone we love. But despite the best of intentions, we often miss the point. All we need, friends, is you. That's it. Your connection. That's all. To hold space for the hurt to heal, to calm, to regulate. Just you and connection.

Think, just for a moment, about when, in this lifetime, you've been the saddest. Sink into that for just a moment. What did you need from other people at the time? We realize instinctually we needed someone who understood. Someone who didn't try to fix it with empty phrases or clichés we hear (and often say) like, "She's in a better place" or "At least you could get pregnant" or, "It was God's plan" (P.S. here's an important tip—*never* use the words "at least" when you're trying to support anyone through grief). But what did you really need? People often tell me they needed "connection," or "just a hug," or anyone to acknowledge the loss and to be less concerned with "making it better." See, we know this to the core of us when we are the griever.

What happens when you're on the other side of grief though? The supporter to the griever. Remember, you've been on one side, you know what you needed when you were the sad one; however, we question ourselves repeatedly when we're on the other side. We doubt what we should do. We question our next move. How many times have you heard people ask each other, "I wonder if I should bring over food?" or, "Should I call or wait?" And we think ridiculous things like, "I don't want to ask her to lunch because it'll remind her of her loss." Sound familiar?

Think back to the "good old days," when we heard of the death of a neighbor. Folks would bring over whatever food they could spare, they packed up all the kids in the car, and off they went to bring comfort in the form of their presence. You took over a musical instrument if you owned one, and booze if it was acceptable. You went directly there, not pausing to wonder if it might be a "bad time." And the children were at your feet when you laughed and cried, ate and drank. They were there watching, listening, and learning what it looked like to make sense of hard things. They were getting the script of what it meant to mourn and heal.

Grief Versus Mourning

Understanding the difference between grief and mourning is one of the biggest insights to ever hit my soul. The wise Dr. Alan Wolfelt,[82] grief counselor and educator, explains the difference like this:

> *Grief is what you think and feel on the inside after someone you love dies. Mourning is the outward expression of those thoughts and feelings. To mourn is to be an active participant in our grief journeys. We all grieve when someone we love dies, but if we are to heal, we must also mourn.*

All of us experience grief. It's something you cannot avoid. We all respond and deal with it differently. The key, for me, is how we mourn. And we're not born with the skills to mourn. We must watch other people do that in order to learn.

Back in the world of trauma, let me remind you that **you can't give away something you've never received**. This is so, so true when we talk about grief and mourning. Someone has to show you how to do mourn in order for you to know what to do in times of sadness. They cannot tell you how to mourn. It's a felt sense. They must show you and you must discover that sense for yourself.

Ceremony

It feels a little much to be discussing funerals in a book for educators, but I think it's important because traditionally, funerals (or wakes or celebrations of life) are ceremonies where many of us have learned some semblance of what it looks like to mourn. Remember how I said the most significant problem we face these days is we have never been more disconnected? This appears to be playing out in how we end our time here on the planet too.

The purpose of a funeral (or a wake) or a celebration of life, represents the very essence of when words aren't enough. Ceremony is a coming together to remind us we are not alone in our darkness and that our broken heart is connected to every other heart that has also known pain. It seems, however, more and more often these days some people are opting to not have a service. Opting out of having a ceremony is concerning. Firstly, in my humble opinion, the person making the decision to not have a funeral or celebration should not be the only one in charge of that decision. Once they die, they're no longer here (wise, aren't I?). Seriously, though, the purpose of the ceremony is for those of us left behind, those of us who are trying to make sense of this hard, but universal, thing by grieving and mourning.

I've also heard concern about taking children to funerals, or to shield them from the pain of death by not involving them in the process for fear that they will "not be able to handle it." I understand the desire to protect our babies from hard emotions or seeing us cry, but it's important for our babes to learn the script of how to mourn by watching the big people in their world go through it. Kids can handle grief. They need a template for how to do this. It's our job to show them.

It's also beneficial to talk with your children about grief in our classrooms. For some, school might be the only place where a kid can talk about death and grief, when the big people in their world are also struggling with the same death, particularly if the death is unexpected or tragic. Big people are often dealing with their own sadness and have some difficulty also attending to their children.

I appreciate, believe me, just how hard this can be in the moment. It becomes our first instinct to protect and "armor up." The excuses about why I shouldn't connect come up much quicker than all the reasons I should. Let me tell you about the time I learned the epitome of this little lesson.

Jillian

Important lessons often come in the midst of big emotions. One of mine came through a profound loss to our dearest friends. I met Colleen when our now-husbands (who were friends) introduced us. Colleen and I were both new to the city and we became connected quickly. Our lives would take parallel turns: We got engaged within weeks of each other; they got married in May and our wedding was in July of the same year. We both honeymooned in Italy (but not together—that would've been weird); when they announced their first pregnancy to us, we surprised them (and ourselves, to be honest) when we found out six weeks later we were pregnant too.

We spent a lot of time together during the growing of our first babies, talking mostly about what it would be like to be moms, comparing our symptoms and our rate of gain (a cow term that my husband often awesomely used throughout my pregnancy). We commiserated about how hard it was to be pregnant. Neither of us knew whether we had a boy or a girl on board and we were protective over our name choices, just in case there was the odd chance that we loved the same one. I was hoping our babies would be fast friends. Colleen was due in June, I in September.

It was a sunny day on June 28, 2010, when the phone rang and I heard Aaron's voice coming from the little back deck of our tiny first apartment. I waddled out there when I heard his voice suddenly change. When I saw Aaron's face, I knew something was wrong. Very wrong. I got that breath-knocked-out-of-you feeling you get when you know whatever is happening on the other end of that call is going to alter the trajectory of life. As I mouthed to him frantically, "What?! Who is it?" he mouthed back, "It's Lon" (Colleen's husband). Then he said "No!" and welled up with tears.

I was wearing a blue t-shirt that day. I will never forget that moment. Me and my big belly dropped to my knees and wept. Colleen could not speak, her husband said, so he didn't give her the phone. We hung up and sat on the deck of that apartment for hours and cried. They named her Jillian.

Colleen had labored beautifully at home with Lon and her doula. When she went into the hospital, despite multiple efforts, Colleen couldn't deliver naturally and a C-section was ordered. As they were awaiting the procedure, delayed due to another emergency in the hospital, something went wrong. Colleen later told me there was no panic in the delivery room until their daughter was out. They worked on her endlessly, it seemed. But their healthy baby girl, at full gestation, had been stillborn.

Days passed with endless questions. Although I called and texted, for two weeks Colleen didn't call or text back. Lon explained that Colleen had been released from the hospital but wasn't ready to see anyone. They both have beautiful families who stayed close. Two weeks after Jillian died, Colleen told her husband, who told my husband, who told me, it would be "okay" if I came over. She hadn't seen any of her friends yet but asked if I could come. "Me??" was literally my first thought. "Why would she want to see *me*?"

I can't even begin to tell you the endless thoughts that circulated in my head, and I'm embarrassed by the number of excuses my mind prepared, almost immediately, for why I couldn't go. I didn't want to see her face. Before I could even leave my house, I spent an hour in my closet trying to figure out which shirt didn't make me look (8 months) pregnant. I didn't want her to remember I was pregnant. That would break her heart, right? I stopped to buy popcorn (of all things) and lamented for 30 minutes about whether to get the cheese, or the plain, ruling out any flavor that had a hint of pink (seriously, WTF!?). When I walked up their front steps, I will always remember the popcorn hitting the floor as soon as I saw her. And after a very long cry and asking everything I could think of about her baby girl, we talked about how we would remember her. And you know what? This incredible mama noticed I was pregnant. We even talked, in this most tender time, about how we would handle it when and if my baby arrived. It was a day I will never forget. Jillian's mama reminded me so much about grief that day, and in the days and years that have followed. More importantly, I learned what it means to mourn.

Jillian would have been eight this year, just like our son Asher, who was born 52 days after Jillian's birth. Jillian's parents held a ceremony for her months later and they celebrate her every year on June 28. And you know what else is cool, one year later we all rejoiced when their second daughter, Chloe, was born. And back to our parallel traditions, when we were on a couple's trip two years later, we shared we were pregnant again. And guess what? So were they! Their son Lucas and our twins were born five days apart. Our six babies will always be part of a bigger magic that reminds me of Brené Brown's words: "Rarely does a response makes something better. What makes something better is connection." Don't you ever doubt it for a single second that connection matters. Sometimes all it takes is a moment. All we want to know is you remember. You look and you see. And I matter.

Our First Response

Bring on the Armor

Just like in trauma, if left to our own devices our first response to grief tends to be to "armor up." To shut down. To tell others "we've got it" or "we're fine." We question whether people need us. We avoid saying the name of the dead one. We think ridiculous thoughts, as I did about Jillian, that doing so will remind them of their loss. Just like with trauma, the most significant thing required in the process of mourning is connection. To lean on others to make sense of hard things, to brave the waves of grief.

Another wise mama I know and love, who faced a terminal illness at the tender age of 42, taught me something else about mourning. She said there is nothing brave about grief. It comes on like a wave and there isn't a damn thing you can do about it. If given the choice, you wouldn't be on that ride. She didn't think it was brave at all that she was the one who had been "blessed" with cancer. As we talked about what it might mean to leave her babies on this planet sooner than she ever dreamed she would, what we talked about, for long hours, was that bravery comes from riding the waves. In the mourning. The bravery comes in not shutting your eyes during the rough seas but keeping them wide open while braving the waves. Trusting that eventually, the waves will pass. And you will always be left with something good. My sweet Rhea, I will be forever indebted to you for this hard and holy lesson.

Grief in the Classroom

Some Things to Consider

A month will not go by, I am told, without having a student lose a pet, or a friend, or something very important to them. All of these experiences are preparing them for making sense of harder things, and how to handle them. We're writing the script for them and need to do it without fixing it all. Hold off, as often as you can, from saying words like, "Your fish is now in a better place" or, "At least Rudy the cow doesn't have to suffer anymore" or, "That's the purpose of 4-H," and especially hold off from saying, "Look on the bright side, kiddo, now you have steaks and hamburger in the freezer!"

When it comes to anyone who has just experienced loss, often slowing things down, getting down on the same level, saying their name, and making eye contact helps to regulate another. We will talk more about that in Chapter 6. For now, remember that when we are regulated, we can make sense of hard things.

Braving the Waves with Your Students:

1. Acknowledge you know about the loss. Sometimes we think because kids don't bring it up, we don't want to cause them any undue stress. You will not remind them. The more significant the loss, the more likely that is to be true.

2. Give other students in the class a "script" for how to respond. Like us, they freeze and don't know what to say or how to respond (without having a model). Walk them through it. A long explanation usually isn't required; however, as long as the experience is a public one, assuring them that connecting with their fellow classmate (who experienced the loss) is okay to do can sometimes be all the permission they need.

3. Stay connected to the big people in the child's world who are most likely also grieving. Being "eyes on" in a different environment may allow the caregivers at home to be aware of what their babe might not want to demonstrate at home for fear of making others sad.

4. Allow outlets for expression—again and again. Things like drawing or coloring for younger children allow them to express feelings they don't yet have words for. If older children or teens don't want to talk about it, suggest they write a letter to you (or someone else) about the hardest parts. Taking a step away from the loss might make it a safer place to identify and clarify their confused feelings. Even more

importantly, encourage them to express the best things or their best memories, as well as the hardest parts, they have about their loved one.

5.   Don't try and fix it. It's natural, and you will be compelled to try. Remember in Chapter 2 how we talked about "Whenever possible, follow the need"? We need to remember this again. We will want to offer suggestions or strategies to make them feel better. We may say things like, "at least mom is not suffering anymore" or, "now grandpa is in a better place." What kids will need, more than anything (just like you and me), is for someone to hear about their pain. The "tell me more" cue often comes in handy if babes start to talk about loss. Just listen.

6.   Acknowledging becomes very critical, particularly if you have to remove a desk or move a locker space. Usually following a student or teacher death, we want to bring in counselors to help kids make sense of hard things. An important thing to consider is to make sure your students like the counselor enough to want to talk. Consider pairing an outside counselor with a well-liked teacher to introduce them to the students. This can make a significant difference.

In the event that a student has lost a parent or direct caregiver, it's always okay to say the parent's or caregiver's name. When Father's Day and Mother's Day comes along, it's okay to make cards for them because they will always be their parent. Mitch Albom[83] wrote, "Death ends a life, not a relationship." These words have become a lighthouse for me in every loss I experience.

CHAPTER FIVE
Game Plan Highlight Reel

1. If you're old enough to love, you're old enough to grieve.

2. There is a big difference between grief and mourning. Grief is what we feel inside after someone we love dies. We have very little control over this—it comes in waves and often unexpectedly. Mourning is how we heal. You're not born with the skills to mourn; you have to be shown how to do this.

3. Mourning often involves a connection with others. Ceremony is an integral part of mourning.

4. As Mitch Albom says, "Death ends a life, not a relationship."

5. In this chapter, you'll find a playbook of a few things I hope will be helpful when you walk through grief and mourning with those you teach, lead, and love. Grief is a universal experience, friend. You can't fix it, but you can help heal.

So, now it is time to start talking about you! What can we do that might be helpful to change a culture that doesn't put self-care first? How can we look after each other so we can look after our babies? One more chapter about what we can do to be helpful for the ones we teach, lead, and love, because knowledge is also self-care. And then it's all about you. Read on. . . .

CHAPTER FIVE

Grief

This grief thing, I'm telling you, we need to talk about it more. When hard things come, though, we would prefer to armor up and hope (often desperately) that the hardest parts are over, that we will be fine. See, the thing is, you will get through it. I promise. I will also promise you this: The waves will come again. It's how this grief thing rolls. My most profound appreciation of grief came when I learned the difference between grief and mourning. That is my biggest hope for this chapter, that you can appreciate the difference between these two and what it means to show someone how to mourn.

1. On that note, discuss what the difference is between grief and mourning. How, if at all, has this understanding changed your perception of this universal process of loss?

2. What do you think is most important for kids to know when they experience loss? How often do the children in your circle—either at home or at work—get opportunities to make sense of grief?

3. Mitch Albom's words, "death ends a life, not a relationship," changed my life. Share how this might help you approach students experiencing grief differently.

THE 5 KEYS TO (RE)CONNECTING

THE ANSWER: GETTING HEARTS AND TAKING NAMES

The quick reference chapter when you feel like you want to throat punch someone

We Are Wired to Do Hard Things

That's a universal truth. When we doubt if we're wired to do hard things, we can look to those who came before us. Many, many people before us, and on this planet at this very moment, are enduring incredibly difficult circumstances. It's easy to lose sight of that when we get caught in our own pain and worry. We would have a hard time saying to someone like Martin Luther King Jr., for example, "We know the fight for civil rights was hard and all, but you have no idea what it's like teaching in small town Alberta these days." Or, "Sorry Viktor Frankl, we know almost losing your life and watching many of your family die in Auschwitz was rough, but 'kids these days' are awful here in Canada." See, we come from a long line of people who have done hard things. We're wired for it. Those hard things are easier to endure when we remember that we're wired for connection. Humans are not solitary creatures. We cannot make sense of hard things alone for long, particularly when those hard things are happening to us or someone we love.

When we experience pain, or fear, or hurt, our prefrontal cortex goes into protective mode and we "armor up." Fight, flight, or freeze takes over and is sometimes our only option. This primitive piece typically serves us well when we're under attack or need to respond immediately. When we need to walk through hard things and stay connected, a regulating other is usually required to keep our prefrontal cortex on to remind us of the important thing: We can do hard things. Often the most helpful, important, and sometimes bravest thing we can do in times of pain and fear is to "lean in" to connection.

Assume with me we're wired to do hard things. And you might be convinced we're much better at doing hard things if we have someone who can help us regulate. How does this apply to kids, you ask?

Think back to the kid who you're most worried about in your world, right now. What do they look like when they're regulated and calm? Let's pretend you have taken away a privilege from that kid, like recess, for example. Pretend this kid is eight years old. You have this babe miss recess today because she was unable to "make a good choice" and she hit some other kid on the playground yesterday. In an effort to teach this kid how to make a good choice, we withdraw a privilege. We have been taught that we take away something she loves in the hopes she will realize our unkind gesture should magically make her want to be kind in moments of distress. Let's say we have her miss recess for six consecutive recesses. When we feel that "isolated time" has effectively taught this babe to be kind, we review the "plan" for when things are going to get tough out there on the playground. Many kind educators around this planet have had discussions that sound like this: "Okay, kiddo. Look at me. When you go back out on the playground today and Jaxon calls you a name, or says you can't play on the swing, what are you going to do?" This kiddo, who is smart, says in a well-practiced voice, "I'm going to take deep breaths, tell an adult, and use my words." She knows the answers right now, see, because she's calm. She has access to everything she's learned (including what you have taught her). In this moment she's kind and thoughtful. What happens, however, when she goes out on the playground, and 37 seconds later, Jaxon calls her a name? She flips her lid and does *not* do everything you just practiced! These "bad choices" leave us confused and feeling like we're never going to get through to this kid.

When you're standing calmly in front of her and you're connected to each other, she has access to everything she's been taught. You love "this side" of the kid. What happens, however, when this very same kid has flipped her lid? My guess is sometimes, when they get dysregulated, they become unrecognizable. I know that to be true with my own kids. Some days when we're in the middle of an epic meltdown, I can't believe we made those sweet babes. I get convinced I will be the only psychologist in Canada to have to explain how all three of my kids ended up in jail. Or how I ended up in there! And then, in the next few seconds, my heart almost explodes as I watch one of them rub the other's back. This journey. It is a tough one.

So, the question is: How do we get compliance (in a way that fosters connection) for the babes who need us? How do we get their prefrontal cortex back online after they flip? Most likely you're already a rock star at this. If you've spent any time in this business of helping other people's children, you know how to regulate others. You're usually much better at this with other people's children, like a kid who is not in your class, or who you don't have much "skin in the game" with most of the time. This, by the way, is why grandparents are often so much "better" as grandparents than they were as parents (in our memories anyway). When you've less to lose, you have greater access to your prefrontal cortex and a whole lot more tolerance, patience, kindness, and insight.

Connection Before Direction

To me, it all comes down to "connection before direction." In other words, the secret sauce is all about regulating first, before you try and teach. The kicker is that connecting is the hardest thing on the planet to do, especially when it's needed the most. It requires us big people in charge to also have access to our prefrontal cortex, because if we don't, we lose the skill, insight, and training we've acquired to do it well for the babes we love and teach (especially the super hard ones). A further hurdle is this connection-first approach flies in the face of all behavioral reason. The consequence/reward model is how so many of us have been taught. And previously, strict behavioral interventions worked so much better in a culture that was connected by proximity to one another. When we widen the physical space between us, it means we pay the cost of co-regulating. Because of that, connect first. And then teach. We've long been taught that consequences must be immediate, and they must "match the crime," otherwise they will carry no meaning. This is true, when we are talking about dogs or rats; however, this isn't true when we're talking about humans. In fact, we can't make sense of a consequence or be taught a single thing when we're dysregulated.

Getting Hearts and Taking Names

I created this handy section for you to go to on the tough days. These are the **5 Keys to (Re)Connection** for the days when you start to think you must have the kid who is exception to all the rules. Now let's be clear: You already have these skills. These are not skills you need to develop. You're so good at this stuff already—when you have no skin in the game. When we're talking about someone else's children, or when you're trying to win over someone's affection, or when you're working with a child who has no language yet, you're so, so good at these skills. This is simply a reminder to do more of what you know to be true. Take a deep breath and give these some thought. By the way—I'll let you in on a secret—they work for everyone. We can use these 5 to help marital couples reconnect, for cops to connect with bad guys, and for leaders to influence their teams.

The Five Keys to (Re)Connection (with anyone in your life)

1. Show Genuine Interest in Things They Care About. First.

When you're in a place of giving your full attention to another, and you have very little invested, or very little to lose, you can go "all in." This isn't a new concept. Getting excited about something that might not have any place in your heart is a primary message used in the corporate leadership teachings or negotiation work. Findcommon ground, they say. They (whoever "they" are) have known this to be true for a long time. If people find you likable, if people feel noticed, heard, or more importantly feel a connection to you, they will be significantly more inclined to learn from you, to follow direction from you, to take direction from you, or to fall in love with you.

The easiest way this makes sense to me is to think about it in terms of cows. Think about going on a first date with someone who you were particularly enamored with, and maybe even with the person you married. Do you remember being interested in things with them that now, in retrospect, you have very little interest in? For me, it was cows. My husband is a feedlot nutritionist. He has a PhD in animal science. He has judged livestock all over the world. In the beginning, I thought that was so cool. I was interested in what he knew. He was so smart and so passionate about the agriculture industry, and still, to this day, I haven't met a wiser man. Secretly, however, even at that time, I had no desire to halter break a heifer. But I pretended I did. When he asked, "Do you want to check cows with me at 3:00 a.m."? What could be funner? Of course, I want to! Do you want your own pair of Carhartt coveralls? Abso-friggin-lutely! Now, friends, sadly the truth must come out: I am scared of cows. I don't like cows. And I'm okay (totally okay) if we don't own any. Ever. But see, at the time, I was aimed at winning his affection. And I knew talking about what he was passionate about was the direct route to his heart. If I came out of the gate with "Eeeeww—cattle? Seriously. That's so redneck. I'm allergic," we likely wouldn't have had a second date. When we feel like our partners aren't interested in what we like to talk about, we stop being interested in their passions too.

It works the same with kids. And anyone we love, really. When you show genuine interest, they can feel it. And the genuine part is where most of us get stuck. How do you do that when the thing they love is Fortnite? Or AC/DC? Or something you find repulsive? Enter that little word that permeates most everything powerful in life: **empathy**. When you can step into someone else's shoes, temporarily, and see their love for something through their eyes, it becomes so much easier to love it too—or at least to understand it. It doesn't mean you condone it, but understanding is the common ground required for anyone to feel heard.

Let's pretend your sweet muffin of love, who is now 16 years old, has started smoking weed. You're adamantly opposed to his choice for a multitude of reasons. First, he has no money, so you're not sure where he's getting it to buy weed. And second: This is your friggin' kid!? He has potential. And he's pissing it all away to get stoned? And he has the audacity to argue about the virtues of pot? You start to try and make sense of it all. How could this happen, you think. Clearly, he takes after the rough side of the family. Then you start envisioning him moving back in with you, with a criminal record, when he's 45 years old and homeless.

If any of this sounds familiar, I'm going to ask you to shift gears for a minute, to do what I like to refer to as my least favorite activity on the planet: Slow it down. Pot is his love. I know, ridiculous even as I write it—but for him, it's important. For him, if I recall being 16 years old (sweet Jesus), I remember the excruciating desire to fit in and be liked. To be cool. Back then, it was Boss t-shirts and a mickey of Sour Puss liquor, which seems minor compared to what kids these days are faced with navigating. The motivations that drive the behavior, however, are universal: to be connected to something or someone.

What do you do in a time like this? If at all possible, take a deep breath and start with those three powerful words we learned about in Chapter 2: **Tell me more.** "Tell me about how it's so much better for you than alcohol. Tell me more about needing it every night to help you sleep. Tell me more about it being so hard to fall asleep these days, son. What's going on?"

And then, once this connection has been established, if you're inclined you can step back into your shoes and start the education process. Now, and only now, does the potential exist for being heard. **Connection before direction.**

2. Get Their Eyes and Say Their Names.

Your second key is eye contact. Eye contact sounds so simple, so mundane. It's a wonder it even made "the list" of critical things. Also, eye contact can be a controversial thing. I have heard many times about the importance of cultural sensitivity when it comes to "eye contact." More specifically, people from certain cultures don't make eye contact because it's disrespectful (e.g., in some First Nations cultures, if you respect an elder or someone in authority, you do *not* meet their eyes). There's certainly truth to that. And what I also believe to be true is your eyes are the window to the soul. When you're sad, devastated, traumatized, struggling with anxiety or grief, where are your eyes? Where are the eyes of many kids in the hallways of a high school? Often under hoodies or behind hair and looking at the floor. This is also true if you're a person who comes from generations of abuse and/or neglect; you too will struggle with making eye contact.

From a (simplified) neurological perspective, when you look at someone and see them, your prefrontal cortex is required. You start to process things like their response to you, judgments about your safety and theirs, whether they know you or just need something from you, what they expect from you, and how they feel about you. Now, it would be weird if you walked into your classroom tomorrow and stared directly and intensely into the eyes of every kid. But how do we make an effort to reconnect when we are usually in our heads thinking about all the things we're missing, or should be doing? The result, friends, is that we miss everything in the moment. I talk to educators about doing this every day so they can connect with their students: **Meet your students in the morning, greet them with their name, and notice whether they give you their eyes.** The ones who do make eye contact easily concern me far less than the ones who don't.

Think about the last time you went through a drive-through. How often do you look into the eyes of the kid handing you your coffee or your burger? How often do you use their name? The handy thing is they all wear name tags, so you have instant access to what everyone in their world calls them. A powerful way to get someone's prefrontal cortex back on is to use their name. This is particularly helpful when you can't get their eyes or when you are physically separated from them (like on the phone).

The eyes of your most sincerely loved ones are sometimes the hardest to hold. Especially when there's a story that makes it difficult. Let me tell you about one of mine. For the past eight years, I have had a hard time holding eye contact with of either of my parents for long. It's not hard to look at them—I love them both dearly—but it is hard to truly "see them," because doing so breaks my heart. I grew up the oldest of two children (my brother is three years younger). My parents got divorced when I was in my second year of college. I don't remember much of that year, but my roommate Rhea told me I cried a lot while on our phone. Those were difficult years. I loved my mom dearly. And I longed to know my dad better. He worked a lot when I was a kid, built amazing things in an effort to provide for us. Mom made up for it with extra love. Their breakup left a hole that never quite made sense to me—until February 2010.

Aaron and I were married and expecting Asher in August 2010. My mom and my stepdad still lived in the house where I grew up, my brother and his family lived a few miles up the road, and my dad had a house in town. Mom suggested I come home for the weekend and since Aaron was away, I was all in. That Saturday morning, Mom and I were at the kitchen table having coffee, when Dad and my brother walked through the back door, into the kitchen, and sat down. My brother and I exchanged glances about this seemingly pre-planned meeting. Then it got weird when Mom brought out lemon loaf (the universal sign of death), brought us all coffee, while Dad continued to joke about something—he's always good at the humor stuff. I relaxed into the conversation, thinking it was weird, but also kind of nice. Mom and Dad had always remained cordial—a feat that always made me proud of them—but even this was a little much.

Then, Dad started to cry. And so did Mom. I knew it—here it is, that trajectory-changing moment. I prepared for a hundred scenarios in the ten seconds that it took Dad to start talking. Clearly, I thought, he had months to live and I wondered if he would ever meet our baby. Or maybe it was Mom? Not Mom. Oh God. And then he said, "Kids, there's something we need to tell you that we haven't told anyone in 40 years." Forty friggin' years?! You've been dying for 40 years, I thought. That can't be right. What else could they have held for 40 years? Dad's gay? In the short time it took me to construct the 100 possibilities, Dad said, "When your mom and I were 18, we got pregnant. We had to give up the baby for adoption. You have a sister. And she's found us."

What. In. The. Sweet. Mother. Okay, first—that's all? I just have a sister? Thank God. I can deal with someone who is alive as long as I don't have to deal with someone dying. I think. But wait just a second. We have a sister? Like a full sibling? Then my brain kicked into overdrive. The questions came fast and furious. When did you know about her? I mean, when did she connect with you?

They started to explain that she was "amazing," that they'd both met her, and learned she'd been raised only two hours from where we grew up! She has a degree in psychology, she is so funny, and her adoptive parents are lovely, and they named her Valerie. When the government unsealed adoption records in 2004, Valerie searched for her biological parents and found us.

Okay. Hold up. A minute ago, I was the only daughter, and the oldest. Now I'm a middle child?? WTF?! So, when they asked the next question, I certainly wasn't all in: "Would you like to meet her?" At first I was thinking, of course I would like to meet her, like potentially next Christmas, when I had a bit of time to process it all. But before I could speak, my brother answered for us. He said, because he's nicer than me, "Of course, Dad, we would love to meet her." Then my father said, "Good. She's in the garage."

The moments that ensued, which involved a lot of staring at each other, crying, talking, a blur of a dinner, and now a whole eight years in between, have been a beautiful mess. We realize how lucky we are. Not all adoption stories turn out this way. For me, the hardest parts are looking into the eyes of both my mom and dad. As a mother, I cannot imagine holding my first-born for only 20 minutes, never seeing her again, and then holding my next baby girl who looks just like the first one, five years later, and not talking about it for 40 years. It breaks my heart because I don't tolerate their broken hearts very well. I want to fix them. And it took me two years to get the courage to ask my dad, "Did you love Mom, or did you just marry her because you felt guilty?" I knew then that I would know the answer if I looked at his eyes. His response? He looked me squarely in my eyes and said, "I loved your mom very much, but you can't hold a secret for that long and not let it destroy you."

Deep breath. Eye contact is the ultimate connection. There's such a big, big difference between looking at someone and "seeing" someone. Have you ever looked at someone you loved, really looked at them, and noticed they had aged? Or that their face looked different than you remembered. Although you interact often, when you truly see them, you notice things about them you might have missed for a long, long time.

See, when people look us in the eye and call us by name, our prefrontal cortex is on as we try and establish how we know you. That's all we need to change the world. More engagement of the prefrontal cortex. That's where our goodness lives. That's where we have access to the people we truly are and want to be. Staying in that space more often will allow us all access to be our best human.

3. Get Down on Their Level.

Number three is magic—another one that is so easy to do, and many people tell me they have forgotten how powerful this simple step can be, but meeting someone face-to-face is where the magic lies. Fear-based techniques were all the rage and still are the ones we refer to in times of significant distress. Does intimidation work? Absolutely. When it's critical I get information from you, I can threaten your life or inflict significant pain, and you will talk. We have come to understand, however, that the information provided is not always as reliable as when you are calm and have more access to your prefrontal cortex, but nonetheless, you can usually evoke a response.

Being on the same level as the other person allows for easier access to their eyes. It slows you down too, because you're consciously thinking about creating an optimal environment. It's quite magical when you can get someone to sit down with you during a yelling match. If you're the parent or educator of a teenager, people often tell me their best conversations happen in a car. You're on the same level. And, they are locked in, which is always helpful! (Just kidding. Not really).

I remember this one time (not at band camp) when I was working at the Children's Hospital, I was supposed to be doing a "fun activity" with a little dude who'd been admitted the previous week for "extreme behavior and violence." I was supposed to assess him during his first week and I also knew I needed to get to his heart somehow. I heard a rumor that the kid liked to cook. I asked him if he had ever made cookies, and he told me that one time he helped a staff member (at a previous group home) make cookies. I wondered if he wanted to try again; he reluctantly agreed. Jesse was ten. He'd been living with his biological mother on and off in between spending time in foster care. He'd blown out of two different schools and was sent to us for a "diagnostic assessment." No one liked this kid and, in fact, many adults were fearful of his "violence" and "quick temper" that just "comes out of nowhere." I offered to get to know the kid in a pompous effort to "model" what it meant to connect with a kid; I proudly marched with Jesse into the kitchen area of our unit.

Jesse willingly came into the baking deal, but had his own ideas—particularly when it came to cracking the eggs. I thought things were going well, until he wanted to crack another egg and I told him we had enough. A discussion ensued, and he ran with the egg he was holding. In my best therapist voice (we have those actually—all soothing and calm), I said, "Buddy, we can't have too many eggs, or our cookies won't turn out." "Fuck you!" he replied and fired an egg at my right boob. And then he ran.

It was a locked inpatient unit so I knew he wouldn't get far. But walking out after him, with raw egg dripping down the front of my (white!) shirt, I could see the eyes and the glances of my colleagues that said, "Easier said than done, hey, psychologist who just writes the plans and never carries them out. . . ." I will never forget how badly I wanted that kid to just listen and sit down (and to stop making me look like a fool!).

I caught up with Jesse, who had attempted to barricade himself in his room. Suggestions about calling security were offered, and I thought about how easy that would be. I could retreat with the excuse that my shirt needed to be tended to, and hopefully someone could calm down this kid. Damn this whole attachment stuff! It takes so much time! Instead, my (now drying) egg stain and I slid down the wall outside of Jesse's room and I sat on my bum. I explained to the onlookers that we were fine (for now) and that I would do my best to regulate and then repair with the kid.

I spoke to Jesse through the door, telling him I was there, and I had nowhere else to be (which was so friggin' untrue it pained me. I had six overdue reports and three unreturned calls, and another two kids to assess that day alone). But I also had the luxury of making Jesse my priority. I wondered as I sat there how many times this kid had felt like a priority. How many times people waited on him, after he had made a stupid choice, and helped him make sense of it. And, as it often did, the answer broke my heart. Now, as you can imagine, Jesse did not make it easy that day. He told me to "Get fucked; go fuck yourself; and fuck off" repeatedly (my personal favorite trio of F-word variations). Eventually, Jesse allowed me into his room, where I sat on the floor beside him. I learned a whole bunch about that dude that day, all from the floor of his sterile locked inpatient unit room, where he and I sat for the next hour. And then you know what? We baked those damn cookies, and they were good. No consequence required.

4. Feed Them and They Will Come.

Speaking of cookies, this leads me to number four. This is probably my most favorite section in the book because food is one of my favorite things in the whole world. Next to my kids. And my husband.

Any my parents (because they're reading this)—but really, food is right up there.

Here's the deal with food: You cannot chew and swallow when your lid is flipped. It's biologically impossible.[84] You would choke. You need your prefrontal cortex to be in place to swallow. Think about the last time you were the maddest you've ever been—mad enough you couldn't speak. You might have even considered punching something (or someone). Did you ever think to yourself, "I just want a sandwich right now!!!?" And at the other end of the spectrum, when you're sobbing at a funeral, you're not simultaneously slamming down the open-faced egg buns, right? Not because you don't want to necessarily, but you're not eating in that moment of extreme distress because you can't. You'd choke. And so, our brain waits until it is more regulated, and then we eat.

Food and drink can become a critical component of helping the people we love make sense of hard things. Various cultures consider food an important part of their societal fabric. And historically, we gather to break bread during difficult times. Where food lost its impact, I think, is when we started to use it as the reward. When we use food as the reward, we are already assuming regulation. For example, when we use the common "Pee on the potty and you'll get a Smarties" game, our babe is regulated enough to actually pee on the potty (if you have ever seen a dysregulated pee-er, you know they ain't getting no Smarties). Or, we say things like, "Read these three chapters and then you can choose from the treat bin." This is also rewarding already regulated behavior.

Instead, use food and drink *not* as a reward, but as the regulating *strategy*. This can be one of your most powerful tools. And I promise you game-changers, if you add number 4 to your repertoire, you will become a very successful lid-flipper-on-er.

Because we've commonly connected food as the reward or the motivator, it flies in the face of reason that food should be offered in times when kids are making "bad choices," because we fear it might reinforce the negative behavior (i.e., kids will be bad just to get a cookie). I've heard concern from numerous educators that "If you give that kid a cookie just after they've flipped a desk, then everyone will flip desks just to get a cookie." At the risk of creating a desk-flipping mafia of cookie fiends, I'd say it's worth a try.

The last time you really lost it you probably said and did things that at the time seemed like pretty powerful, point-getting-across, kick-in-the-nuts kind of statements. What happened, however, once your lid came back on is that you took a step back when you became regulated again, and often shame, remorse, and guilt bubbled to the surface. We only usually get to that desperate space of flipping our lid when we perceive there are few other options. Despite our efforts, we are still not being heard or understood, so we turn it up. We would not just "go there" to get a cookie. And neither do kids. Now, when kids see other kids getting cookies or water, they might ask about when they get a cookie. See, the cool thing is the asking-kid is regulated. You can reason with him. You can explain that, "Right now, Jaxon needs my help and this cookie is going to get me there." If this kid flips his lid too, then we deal with it in the best way we can, with what we have. Intentionally becoming "flipped" just to get a cookie is not how kids roll.

5. Never leave them—proximity matters—especially when they tell you to go.

We're wired for connection. We're able to settle so much better when we have someone who will regulate with us. We do remarkably better with another person by our side when we need to make sense of hard things. Some call this co-regulation. We have a very, very hard time making sense of things alone. Can we? Sure. Sometimes we need our space. Sometimes we have been given no choice—we have been abandoned. But without exception, how we soothe, calm, and regulate, is always best with the assistance of another trusted, regulated human. Donald Winnicott once said, "There is never just a baby. There is always a baby and someone." We have known this for a long time. Kids cannot make sense of hard things alone for long.

Time-Outs

People often ask me about time-outs and time-ins and I always have the same answer: I am a huge believer in time-outs. For *you*—not (necessarily) for your kid. When we become too exhausted, fired up, or enraged with the response of a child, we have a very difficult time remaining with them. When we flip *our* lids, we do and say things we later regret. Often, though, we have enough in the tank to realize we need a break. A time-out. Sometimes someone else might suggest it (which is generally seldom well received). Regardless, if I'm not okay, my kids don't stand a chance.

Now for the tricky part. I've never heard myself or any other parent say to a babe, "Go to your room. I need a break and so do you," and the babe respond with, "Good idea!" Or, "10-4 mom." If you send them to their room they're usually stomping, kicking, or some form of guttural screaming.

So, my strategy instead is to head to the bathroom. It's the only room with a lock in our house (how did that happen!?). When I get to this point, I either fake having to pee or I say, "I need a minute!" and I go there and lock the door. Quickly, because there's usually one of the three in hot pursuit. In there, just for a moment, I breathe. Just 20 seconds. If it's really bad, I may keep a bottle of white wine sealed in the tank of the toilet because it's chilled, and no one knows it is there. Just make sure you get the screw cap kind (Just kidding . . . sort of).

Seriously, though, often all it takes is a minute or two and I can remind myself that my personally created muffins of love don't have adult brains and they need my help to sort it out. In this moment, they just simply don't know how.

A woman from Guatemala once expressed her confusion to me about how common it is for parents to send their kids to their rooms. In her childhood, she clearly remembers, whenever she was in trouble her mother would hiss the words, "Sit right here near me and don't you move." She wouldn't dare move. This is a clear example of how kids stayed close to the hands on the circle in another culture. Eventually, sometimes even without words, disconnect between the adult and the child would be repaired.

Summary of the Five Keys to (Re)Connecting

They tell me that if you are going to develop keys or lists of things for people, you should also come up with an acronym so they remember it. Makes sense to me—but turns out I'm not awesome at this. I sat with a scratch pad for hours trying to come up with a word that might make sense. Here's the best I got (and I like it because it reminds me of farms. And cows). When you want to be the most outstanding person in your FIELD, remember these things to take into your FIELD every single day. They are all that matter, first, last, and always:

F—Feed them
I—(show) Interest that is genuine
E—(get) Eye contact and say their name
L—Leave them never—especially when they tell you to go away
D—Down on their level is where I want you to be

Your Power with Parents

Educators are Rock Stars to Us

One of the most important things to consider when (re)connecting with people is *who* you're connected (and not connected) with. Now that we've talked about some critical components when reconnecting with kids, I want you to think about also using this magic with their parents. Can I just tell you, sometimes (read: often) your relationship with the parents can be even more important than your relationship with the kids.

We forget the power we have with the parents. As an educator, what you think and what you say matters to us. When you engage with parents and light them up, or reassure them, or acknowledge them or their child, I cannot even tell you the ripple effect this can sometimes create.

Let me tell you about this mama I met one time who was changed by a teacher. This mama drove three hours from a small town in our province to see me, finally arriving at her appointment after being on a waitlist for three months. Her baby was six and was in a public-school division. The only thing I had in the referral was, "We really need to see you. The school diagnosed my boy with autism, and I don't think my son is on the autism spectrum. I am so upset that I have pulled him out this June and will be homeschooling him. I have no experience with teaching, but I have no choice. We just want a bit of a consultation." When she walked into my office that day, she had both her babies in tow (the older one too, who was 10 years old), because she could not afford to have anybody look after them and knew she would not get back home in time to collect her older babe from school.

When I first laid eyes on her boy, I understood why he might be on the school's radar. He had been in our waiting room for exactly 24 seconds and he had crushed all the chewy candies I had in my coveted glass bowl. He went through the toy bin, spread every crayon I had color coordinated across the floor, and was trying to climb up my very fancy IKEA bookshelf. I loved him instantly. Once we wrangled the little dude into my office and gave him a snack, mom came in and sat down. She handed me a thick report and said, "Here's what they said. He's on the autism spectrum. I have done a lot of reading. I don't think he is on the autism spectrum. And last year, after they told me that about my boy, with no explanation, I decided the public system was not for us. I'm homeschooling."

I looked at this mom. I looked at this kid, who was now done with his snack and was crashing toy dinosaurs into each other. We explored all the testing that had been done and I further assessed him. My guess was that she was right and her babe was not on the spectrum; he certainly had significant developmental issues, but autism didn't appear to be one of them. And then I asked her, worried a bit about the answer she would give me, "How's the homeschooling going?" She said, "Actually, he's back in school!" I said, "No way! What happened?" "I just need to tell you," she said, "Last summer before he went into first grade, I decided the school didn't understand my boy. How could I give my baby to a bunch of people who didn't want to understand him? But then, you know what happened? His teacher, Mrs. A, sent my kid a postcard in the summer that said, 'I cannot wait to meet you.' Can you believe that?!" She looked astonished and so very proud. "That Mrs. A—she couldn't wait to meet my boy. Now, that postcard is on our fridge and I'm going to put it in his baby book after this year is over. She's so nice—and he loves her."

A bit stunned at this point, I was thinking, that's all it took? A postcard sent in the mail. I asked her if she'd told Mrs. A just how important that connection was to her. She responded, "No. I didn't tell her. I don't know if it's a big deal." Whereas, I'm thinking Mrs. A is a game-changer!

You see, the reason this woman returned her babe to public school was simply about connection—feeling seen and heard. Of course, public education isn't always the answer—I see many successful families homeschool their children. But this mama was scared, and sad, and protective of her boy (and just so you know, I connected this babe to the local Developmental Clinic so a more thorough assessment could be completed because these advanced assessments are not often available within our school systems). I also asked mom if I could call Mrs. A and she was thrilled that I would do this for her boy.

I called Mrs. A the next day and told her the impact the postcard had on that boy. "I sent one to every kid" she said. "Yeah, I know, but don't tell Mom that. You need to know it's still hanging on her fridge. And it's going in his baby book. And PS—you're phenomenal. You just changed the trajectory of that little boy's life without knowing it. Thank you."

After that one five-minute phone call, how do you think that teacher felt? Is she in the game? Is she going to meet that mama at the door and light up when she sees that boy? You bet. Does that mama have a school she's connected with to help that kid graduate twelfth grade? Absolutely. One postcard.

When the School Calls

Speaking of parents and power, if you're a parent, you know the sometimes gut-dropping feeling you get when the school calls? The call is usually because there's something wrong with your kid, or something needs to be addressed, or you have to come and pick your kid up. These calls, as you can bet, are more frequent for the kids who suck the most from you. The kids who need it the most, as you know, are the hardest to give it to. And that's generally true for their parents too. Parents who are struggling with their babes often question their capacity to parent; however, you may never know it. Sometimes those of us who feel the most incompetent, scared, or unsure can present as the most defensive or standoffish. Armor at its finest. Let me just tell you, dear one, a phone call to Jaxon's dad to say something like, "I just wanted you to know I think your boy is pretty awesome" can change a life. A 20-second phone call can rewrite the story of an entire evening, when a dad expects something bad about their kid and hears from you that they're amazing. You, sweet educator, are so powerful.

One More Little Thing

Let's end this chapter with brutal honesty. We're going to screw this up. A lot. As the big people trying to teach and influence little people, you would be a robot if you got it right all the time. **Remember the 30%.** Responding to the cues of a child 30% of the time with "hands on the circle" is all we need. You've got this. I am sure of it.

CHAPTER SIX

Game Plan Highlight Reel

1. We're wired to do hard things. We know this to be true when we look to the people before us who have survived the most unimaginable hardships.

2. Having the most significant and long-standing influence with anyone in your world always requires a relationship.

3. This chapter includes a playbook for you to refer to when you need to (re)connect to the people in your world. There are five simple

strategies that you do very well, most of the time. They're here now for you, in case you ever forget just how powerful you are.

4. You are so good at connecting to those you teach, lead, and love when you are filled up and supported. I would strongly encourage a budget for meat trays in every division (more on that in the next chapter).

5. Remember your power with the parents of the babes you hold every day. Most often, if you have their hearts, their children's will follow. The ones who need it the most will be the hardest to give it to.

Turns out, I have a few ideas about how we can keep you (and your respective divisions) in the game. It's called the **Carrington Connections Network for Educators** and it's designed to provide school systems with a plan for developing a consistent internal wellness structure that can be used across divisions to hold each other up in the times of crisis. My dream is that this model will be adopted across North America (so we can do a little thing like change the face of education on this continent). But for now, we'll end this sweet little book talking about some specific thoughts just for you, and how we might keep you not only surviving, but growing and loving this holy work you do. You are the key to it all. Read on. . . .

CHAPTER SIX

THE ANSWER: GETTING HEARTS AND TAKING NAMES

This chapter is centered around a little list I created when some-one told me that you need to have useable takeaways for people. Honestly, I don't know how these things made the list. A couple of them are things I want you to think about, while a couple others are practical things I want you to do. What I know for sure about all of them, however, is that they're foolproof. A little bit of one of them or a lot of all of them will always, in all ways, bring you and those you teach, lead, and love to a better place. Use this chapter often. It won't steer you wrong.

1. Do you ever doubt in this life that you are wired to do the hard things? The soul-crushing, heart-breaking, tough ones? (By the way, we all doubt ourselves sometimes.) Share what, if anything, pulls you out of those moment.

2. If you've had a chance to get someone's eyes and say their name (particularly someone you don't know, like a service provider at the airport or at a coffee shop), discuss your funniest reaction. If you haven't tried this yet, see how many people in the span of a week you can get to comment on your engagement with them. (It'll happen. Trust me.) Share your experiences.

3. How do we get around the concern that using food and drink when kids are upset will "reward bad behavior"? Is this still a common perception in your circle? How do you think we start to shift this idea? (Hint: Connect with them about it over a coffee and a meat tray—just a thought.)

GREAT LEADERS BUILD A CULTURE ON RELATIONSHIPS

THE CARRINGTON CONNECTIONS NETWORK FOR EDUCATORS

A Model for School Division Mental Health

Someone once told me it's okay to be motivational. That's kind of the easy part. To drop in and throw around a little sunshine, do a talk, or even a one-day workshop, then leave. And then what? What does it take to be *transformational*? That right there is what gets me fired up! It is time, educators, we stop being just motivational and we start to see this holy work you do every day as transformational. There's no other institution that provides such a vast opportunity to influence our next generation—every single day.

It's easy to talk about how to do things differently, to have **Five Steps to (Re)connection** and strategies to lean on when things get challenging. But what does it take to sustain it once the "inspiration" wears off, when you find yourself back in the trenches and think you're likely the exception to the rule?

Within the world of business and corporate culture, there's a plethora of theories and strategies that guide people. Raymond Dalio,[85] "the Steve Jobs of investing," stresses that "the WHO is more important than the WHAT." He adamantly believes that we need to hire people who are better than we are at their specific job or skill set. Knowing you can put people in places who will do their respective jobs well means you get to sit back and "conduct" rather than "orchestrate" every move. Brené Brown's *Dare to Lead*[86] was released just before this book went to the editor, and I was inspired most by her insights around creating teams using the **Accountability and Success Checklist.** It supports the importance of developing a culture in which people want to work hard for you and can help to revolutionize the historic (and archaic) institution that is our education system in North America.

Great Leaders Excavate the Unsaid

If you're leading anyone—a team of seven-year-old hockey players, a corporate team of lawyers, a group of construction workers, or a school division—your job, as a leader, is to be a regulating other. When you can keep people engaged and feeling worthy, they will work hard for you. People won't work hard if they think you don't like them. End of story. People have died (and killed) for good leaders. Players will play harder, smarter, and without rest for coaches who they believe have their back. They'll be able to do this because in times of distress, doubt, anger, sadness, remorse, you name it, they have someone at the helm who can guide them back to their best. Leaders who have the capacity to sit in the dysregulated times. Just like with kids, telling them to calm down or micromanaging their every move doesn't work. It makes sense why we want to do it sometimes—we want the best from them (and sometimes for them), but you cannot tell someone how to deliver well; you must show them. When you're the leader of people who do hard work, your greatest asset will be to keep them regulated in times of distress. Keep them connected to each other and to the people who love them. When those feelings of dysregulation arise, when you witness or feel that in your team, your sole job is to excavate the unsaid. Just like in a therapeutic relationship, you need to "name it to tame it." Name the emotion or the thing you're not happy with, that doesn't sit right. It's as simple and as complicated as this.

Getting the Culture Right

Imagine working in a team of educators who all want to take on the tough babes. A team who, even on their worst days, remembered they were changing the world. A team who, whatever they had on any given day, believed they were enough. That kids these days are better than they've ever been, and all they need was people to guide them to be their best, particularly when they're at their worst.

The culture or the "feeling" in almost every school I walk into is different. It often doesn't take long before you can feel it and it's often in the little things. One of the most telling observations to me is how students are greeted when I walk down the hallway with any staff, particularly senior administrators or leaders. If students make eye contact with them, if the staff know their names, if they interact with them, even when a stranger (me) is with them, all of that speaks volumes about their connection. How staff greet each other is also another big kicker—the location of admin offices or availability of staff for other staff, including bus drivers, custodians, and EAs. It is engagement (or lack thereof) in the staff room. I often joke about the importance of "meat trays" in a staff room and I always encourage any school leader who will listen that they need a budget for meat trays. Food (good food—not cheap stuff) in a staff room can turn any staff around. I've not seen anything like it: You feed educators and they rise. It's a beautiful thing. At the heart of it all, the "culture" in any school is so critically important.

Jimmy Casas[87] coined the term "**culturize**": "To cultivate a community of learners by behaving in a kind, caring, honest, and compassionate manner." The purpose, he outlines, is to challenge and inspire each member of the school community to become more than they ever thought possible. And it all starts with relationship. What I love most about his innovative read is he highlights the understanding that "everyone is a leader." Today, right here, right now, you have the power to be the change within the culture that is the school where you work. It's important work. It's critical work.

Good Enough Isn't Good Enough Anymore

A mantra like Casas's should be the starting point for an organization that holds our babies. How can you make it happen? How do you start with a team that isn't just happy with mediocre? If you're reading these words, my guess is, this is you. You would love to be in a job where you believe, to the core of you, that you can make a difference in this world. That you wake up every day, often before your alarm clock, because you have found a passion that feeds your soul. Very few people would say, "I would much prefer staying in a job where I can just fade into the background." I have heard people, way too many times, counting their days to retirement, let alone the days until a holiday break. That, my friends, breaks my heart. If you're in that spot, how did you get there? And more importantly, how in the name of all that is holy do we get you back into a place where just "good enough" isn't good enough anymore?

It Starts at the Top

Another cliché that I think deserves attention here is, **"It starts at the top."** Having a solid team who believes they can change the world is always helpful. I want to be clear, however, that starting anywhere is more than worth it. Oftentimes the primary excuse is that "administration" is the problem. And that is sometimes the truth. What's more important, though, is what you have control over in this moment. Right here, right now: **"Relationship knows no hierarchy."** Those at the top have just as much doubt in themselves as some of us at the bottom. They're also susceptible to the power of compliments.

Don't doubt, it ladies and gentlemen: If you're not a senior administrator and are reading these words, stopping in at your division office to give thanks for an initiative you found helpful can shake up an entire system. They (the big shooters) will not know what to do with that. I promise.

And if you are a big shooter who is reading this, your most powerful move is to show up, in person, with a meat tray, and tell your EAs, and custodians, and teachers, face-to-face, that they matter. This will be more powerful in getting productivity and joy than any policy you will ever create or enforce.

The Feedback Loop

Checking in often about how something "lands" with someone who you're leading (or loving) is another powerful tool. Assumptions come way too fast and are easy when we don't often check in, clarify, and make sense of things with the people we lead or love. In this world of disconnect and lack of proximity, texts and emails can divide teams. Face-to-face conversations unite, especially when hard conversations are warranted. **Evaluating accurately, not kindly, is a mantra that I promise will serve you well.**

It's interesting to observe that every school division in every province within Canada has its own unique administrative setup. There's no standard of practice when it comes to the organizational structure of each division. Each province has varying numbers of divisions dictated primarily by geography; however, I haven't been a part of one yet that has the same organizational structure as the next. Some have one superintendent and five directors, while others have assistant superintendents or associates. The teams charged with the physical and mental health of students also have no consistency and are often disconnected from the rest of the divisional team, doing phenomenal work but often in silos. Let me be clear: This isn't necessarily a bad thing if it's working well. However, it's difficult to measure success when there's no consistent approach to leadership or, more specifically, no consistent template to lead the overall wellness of students and staff. As we come to understand very clearly, academic success becomes inaccessible to students who are emotionally unavailable. Even more importantly, the most brilliant pedagogical lesson plans based on the best literacy and numeracy practices (coupled with a whole stack of Chromebooks to deliver this pedagogy) will be completely ineffective if our staff is not emotionally regulated.

Also significant to note is the disproportionate gender ratio in the leadership level of education. It is astounding that despite the fact that nearly 80% of women make up the teaching profession in any given province, very few hold senior leadership positions. As I write this, there are currently 75 public, separate, francophone, and charter school authorities in Alberta, Canada. But only 16 women (22%) hold superintendent positions.[88] Similarly, in the United States, women also far outnumber men at every level of the K-12 career ladder except at the superintendent's level.[89]

There are a number of things about this gender discrepancy that become important as we consider the shift to (re)connecting our staff. The argument that only the most qualified should hold those senior positions is an interesting one. Speaking from a position of purely statistics, wouldn't the likelihood of a qualified candidate be significant when the selection pool is nearly 80% women? I think we need to further challenge the confined heteronormative gender roles that do not "allow" women to take such "demanding" positions in order to disrupt the assumptions around "most qualified." I cannot help but wonder (and hope) if leading by relationship first is the answer, a strategy more often employed by women, if the time is now for female educators to knock those numbers upside down. Remember: **Relationship knows no hierarchy. Relationship knows no gender.**

Organizational Hierarchy in School Divisions

When trying to understand the levels within each school division, understanding hierarchy appeared to be much clearer than the organizational structure of each division. Everyone agrees the kids are where we start. They're the primary focus of each division. The next level is the parents and caregivers. Next comes the educational assistants and support staff, including custodians, bus drivers, administrative assistants, before- and after-school care workers, and librarians. Teachers then take up the next rung. The "Wellness Team" was next (made up of the division's staff who are clinically responsible for the "tough kids" or those with mental health or physical needs). Next level is those in charge of directing each individual school, such as principals and school leadership teams. Depending on the size of the school, there are often committees or teams designated for various administrative tasks that keep a school running well. Lastly, senior leadership teams are often made up of those big shooters who take up residence in the "head office" and are required to report to the Board of Trustees.

Traditional School Division Hierarchy

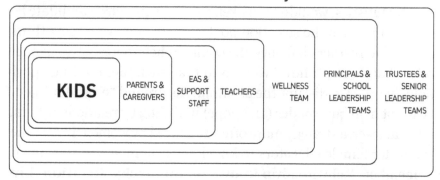

From an organizational administrative perspective, this setup is obviously necessary. There are policies and procedures that need to be allocated and overseen, budgets to adhere to, and government rules to oblige, and not everyone can do the front-line work.

What we now ask, however, is where the bulk of support resources are being allocated. Again, there's universal agreement that the kids receive most of the resources in all areas including educational support (obviously), as well as physical and emotional supports. This had never been questioned because indeed, the kids are the reason we all gather and why this institution of education was created. Staff were clear that "programming" was largely focused on students, including investments in anti-bullying, anti-suicide, self-esteem building, behavioral modification, and career planning supports. But when I ask what resources of support are provided for any of the other "rungs" of the ladder, there was often a significant pause. Front-line staff often say they have potlucks as a team. Potlucks. Nothing says you're appreciated more than "bring your own food!?"

There's also discussion about the professional development required for most staff to attend on a regular basis, but the focus, many agreed, is largely about how better to deliver numeracy and literacy. Very few resources are provided about how to support students through dysregulation, or trauma, or grief. And self-care suggestions for staff are often limited to gym passes and a review of a generic EAP program.

Now, as I write these words, I can almost feel the ire from administrators, from those who have spent their entire careers doing their very best to create systems where staff feel supported and encouraged. Ire from senior administrators who feel connected to their front-line teams, from senior administrators who didn't have students as their primary focus. In my very limited experience to date, the culture in education hasn't been focused in that direction. This is no one's fault. When you know better, however, it's time to do better.

Could it be that it's now time for a shift? What I do believe is the majority of those of you reading this book have rarely felt you were the most important and critical component to the success of students. These educators, at all levels of the administrative hierarchy, are holding my most precious gift for more hours a day than I do. These educators need to be supported just as much (if not more so) than the kids. Good enough is not good enough anymore.

Relationship Knows No Hierarchy

Dream with me just a bit. What would happen, friends, if you walked into schools every day where we're not trying to plan for "triggers and motivators," but instead where there is a team of people who knew how (and were supported) to face those most challenging kids head-on, together? Where common language exists that allows us to stay connected through it all. Where we did our very best to regulate each other, knowing if we do that, we'd have everything we needed to regulate the emotion of the "tough ones" again, and again, and again. If we hope to leave this job with a legacy of healthy students, this simply cannot, ever again, be a one-person job. Every EA, teacher, and bus driver alone cannot succeed (for long) without feeling defeated and overwhelmed. We are much better able to stay passionate about the work when we stay connected and filled up.

Other observations I have noted (if you're still with me, administrators), is that in most divisions, teams responsible for the education of the most challenging students are very disconnected from each other. There's a tendency to keep the important information about emotional well-being and trauma histories silent, under the very real stipulation that it is "confidential." Let me be clear: As a psychologist, no one can appreciate the importance of confidentiality more than I do. I will also tell you, however, that if we expect those of you in the education system to do your job well, and as a connected team, the information needed to provide safe and effective education for a student will involve the ethical and moral necessity for you to know at least *some* confidential information. The ones we worry about the most, the ones who flip their lids the most or fly under the radar, often have a story that, if at least some of you know, will provide your staff with an empathy that will be necessary to walk them through the emotional dysregulation required before they're able to learn. If you're assigned to or interact with this kid on a regular basis, you need to know if they have a trauma history. Full stop. You need to know that they're going to flip their lid and why. Because guess what? That information will help you keep this babe's lid on—oh, and it will help keep your lid on as well, keeping everyone involved safe and supported.

Although every province has their respective information-sharing legislation, as we developed our connection model in Alberta, Canada, we often referred to the Children First Act.[90] This Act serves to govern all of those individuals responsible for children. In brief, a primary element for the Children First Act allows for greater information-sharing between and within agencies that provide care and education for children. This means sharing the sometimes-confidential information among professionals, allowing for the best educational programming for all students. Knowing that a student has a trauma history can help put their behavior into context and allows *all* professionals room for empathy. With the Children First Act comes a professional responsibility, of course. If someone breaches confidentiality, then it becomes an administrative issue. Imagine if all of us who provided transportation or care for a kid like Jaxon, every day, had information about his story, how life-changing might that be?

Let me give you an example. Let's say I approached Harold, who has been the bus driver in our division for the past 18 years, about a "challenging kid" we were about to receive. Harold, as this kid's bus driver, will be the first and last set of eyes on the kid every day. I might say,

> *Harold, do you have a minute? You've been here over 18 years, haven't you, Harold? I need to tell you a little something about Jaxon before he starts with us next week. I don't know everything yet, but here's what I do know. He's new to your route and our school. He's 10 years old and he's likely going to test even your patience. I expect us to have many conversations about this sweet boy who is kind of hard to love. This kid is known for his spitballing skills. Apparently, he can clear the length of two school buses!*

Then I'm going to say to Harold,

> *Here's what else you need to know, in confidence, Harold, because I think it's important for you to have this information. He's in his sixth foster placement within the last five years. This babe has never had a dad figure who has been kind to him. When he gets on the bus in*

the morning, he will not make eye contact. He might flip you the bird. He's angry and disrespectful. And in all honesty, what I know about his story so far, he has every right to be. He might do all kinds of things that are not going to look respectful. Our goal is to keep him here till Christmas. If I can get him on your bus to school every day between now and Christmas, we are going to have achieved a feat that no other school has been able to do. Are you with me on this, Harold? Is this possible? Please know, I fully appreciate that your job is to keep our kids safe, and I want you to do that whenever necessary. I just thought it might help to know a few things about your new kid. And it turns out that he's an Oilers fan!

And Harold—a dedicated Oilers fan who has a huge heart and whose "why" is about helping kids and having coffee at the Legion with his buddies since he retired, might say,

This kid has never had a dad? Like, ever be nice to him? Hrmph. But he's an Oilers fan, so that's good enough for me.

What are the odds of something good happening when Harold picks up this little dysregulated bug the very next morning? Jaxon gets on the bus, hoodie up, eyes down, and Harold says, "Morning, Jaxon." He replies, "Whatever," under his breath (or he'll be in stunned silence like those drive-through workers!). Harold doesn't miss a beat and says, "How about them Oilers! Did you see the McDavid goal last night?" Jaxon might even pause for a moment and wonder if Harold has been drinking. He can't figure out what the hell is going on here. See, you need access to your prefrontal cortex to try to figure out "what the hell is happening?" and consequently, Jaxon is no longer dysregulated. The seeds of connection have been planted.

My job should be to identify who else in Jaxon's "village" might need to know something about our boy. Next up is Ethel—the school's administrative assistant, who, by all accounts, runs a tight ship. I might say,

Ethel, I've got to tell you something about our new kid. You might have noticed him the past few days—always lurking in the hallway. I just needed to tell you a little more about him—this one breaks my heart a little. In confidence, I need you to know that he's been in five foster homes and he is only 10 years old. He often doesn't bring much to school to eat. He's not going to follow the rules very well, but I've got to tell you a little bit about what he loves. He loves Skittles so at Walmart I bought 64 bags of these mini Skittles. Now, I know how busy you are, and I'm so thankful for you. I'm just wondering if you would keep these Skittles packages in your desk and just tell him to stop by at lunch every so often, could you do that for me? I just think if he feels like we welcome him here, we might manage to keep him until Christmas. He's been kicked out of his last two schools. I'm just not going to let that happen here. Are you with me on this? Can you help me on that?

She might reply something like,

You just want me to give him Skittles every once in a while? What does he look like again? Can you show me? He's the kid with the Transformers shirt. . . . Yeah, he's usually quite dirty, and those inappropriate jeans he wears! My goodness!

Our Ethel, who also has six grandchildren and a heart of gold underneath that tough exterior says, "So this kid has not had a dad?" And then you see this woman melt before your eyes and you somehow know that she just might become his biggest fan.

See, I know you could quickly and easily answer when I ask you to give me the top five kids you're worried about in your school right now. There will be quick agreement on who those five are because they're not surprises to anyone. If they're not surprises, then we need to implement a plan about who will be their hands on the circle. Not *how* we're going to stop the behavior, but *how* we're going to support the kid.

Teachers say to me all the time, "I'm here to teach. I'm not here to be a mental health therapist." Yes, hear me when I write that this statement is very true. That's why we need to build teams for those kids and understand the importance of emotional regulation. Then and only then, do you get to do the academic part of your job. You're much more likely to be able to teach in a classroom that has kids who are ready to learn if we pay attention to the lid flippers. As Jimmy Casas and colleagues point out in *Culturize*,[91] everyone is a leader. Reminding staff of that and creating spaces where you inspire everyone starts with relationship. With each other, for each other. Surround yourself with the people on your staff who think like you. Don't start with the tough ones that don't believe as much as you do. This has become my mantra as of late: **Sit with the winners. The conversation is different.**

Leadership in These Times of Disconnect

How to Rock It

Here's the deal—I've left this discussion purposefully to the end because I have no business telling educators how to structure their divisions. I'm not an educator (in case I failed to mention that previously), and there has been a long line of phenomenal research on how to create a pedagogically sound educational system. But what I do wonder about is how to build all that beautiful pedagogy on a bedrock of relationship. I want to create a **culture of connection** that allows the most critical work on the planet to happen. I want a culture of connection in the places where we expect things to go wrong, for crises to happen, and we welcome them because we understand. Because we have a plan. And if we don't, we have a whole slew of other divisions across a country who do.

I'm giving you a model that was created with educators, for educators in the hope this may serve as a guideline, wherever you are in the world, to develop a platform upon which all the programs you currently employ can be built.

The Carrington Connections Network for Educators

A Model for School Division Mental Health

Regardless of the school division, you all do the same hard work. The children, across the country, experience similar issues and have similar stories. And despite having the same big challenges, school divisions, even those within close physical proximity to one another, are very disconnected. Remember, **we are wired to do the hard stuff**—but we are so much **better at handling the hard stuff when we are connected.**

The stories of the most worrisome kids, the school shooters, the suicidal ones, the parents who didn't get it—these are universal.

Some divisions handle it better than others, but I question, why don't all of you offer support to each other?

Inspired by those Bott babies I told you about in the opening pages of this book, the idea of a **Carrington Connections Network for Educators** was formed. It comes with an advisory board of three different school division leaders whom I respect greatly, and it slowly developed into a model designed to answer the "now what?" question. It's a five-stage process that allows for school divisions to first start speaking the same language, to then create sustainability within their respective divisions, and to network with others who have similar training and expertise when (not if) a crisis (big or small) comes knocking. The **Carrington Connections Network** exists so you are never alone in this process again.

A Call to Action

Shifting the Culture at School and Division Levels

We must look after our educators first. This is a philosophical model on which divisions can base their practices and it doesn't replace any programs currently in place within your school board (every division we've worked with has programs incorporated within their schools to address concerns about student well-being). Instead, this model is developed to ensure that all components employed in a division are built on a relationship-based, trauma-informed platform that focuses on staff first.

Here is Our 5 Step Model:

1. Division Consultation

We've come to understand that every division is at a different place in addressing the mental wellness of their staff and students. Our first meeting, sometimes over the phone, with Senior Leadership, is the starting point of our work together. This meeting would be attended by Dr. Jody Carrington and/or a senior education advisor from one of the **Carrington Connections Network** divisions. We are interested in what you've developed and where you think your biggest challenges are. Together we will talk about if and how we might be able to help incorporate any amazing initiatives you already have implemented (such as Leader in Me,[92] the VTRA model,[93] Zones of Regulation,[94] and Collaborative Response Model[95]). We want to be clear that this is not a replacement for anything that you're already doing, rather a philosophical shift from which all staff can move forward and implement many of the amazing things you might already have in place.

2. Senior Leadership Consultation

On a separate day, following the division consultation, we will establish a direction and a partnership necessary to engage administration and school leadership teams in the plan moving forward. The focus of this one-day session is on creating connection and instilling hope within the leaders of your division so they can do that for the staff they lead. In some divisions this involves a day with principals and trustees where we talk about relationship and connection, prefacing the presentation of the plan for your division to address mental wellness. Getting "buy in" at this level is imperative. The idea is to create what Émile Durkheim referred to as **collective effervescence**—the importance of the collective, working towards a clearly defined direction, resulting in a cultural shift toward hope and optimism.

3. Professional Development for All Staff and Parents

The critical key in this first (of three) day-long PD session is that all staff attend. This includes bus drivers, administration assistance, librarians, educational assistants, speech pathologists, occupational therapists, before- and after-school care providers, counselors, and custodians. This day is designed to provide your whole team with a common language of **relationship and connection** and to begin to cultivate the belief that we're in this together, because it truly does take a village to raise a child.

We have also found it extremely beneficial, whenever possible, to invite community partners to this first day of "the basics," particularly those who have frequent interactions with school staff, including Child and Family Services, cultural supporters, local police, and non-profit organizations involved in community programming (e.g., Family and Community Social Services, Early Childhood Coalitions, Boys and Girls Club).

Following this, your staff complete two additional days of PD—one day focussed on **trauma-informed practices** and another day to focus on **compassion fatigue** and **grief**. These can be delivered in short succession or spread over a school year. It's during these days, particularly our first day with your whole staff, that we will introduce the entire plan to shift the culture towards wellness and connection, while instilling hope and optimism. Having more than just one day with your staff provides the message we're in this for the long haul and also provides opportunities for push-back to our team, instead of internally within your respective schools.

There's also a parent evening session. This two-hour event has frequently been co-hosted by community groups and the school. We've found it's critical to educate parents and caregivers about the culture shift that may be happening within your school. More importantly, providing parents with the same "common language" your educational staff will now be speaking, serves to further expand the village for all children, but especially for the ones who need it the most. From a cost-effective stance, this session is often offered on the evening after "the basics" PD session is done with all staff.

4. Clinical Wellness Team Training: Creating Sustainability

Once all staff have received a basic understanding of emotional regulation and the importance of relationship, we will identify, along with your leadership team, who makes up the "clinical team" in your division. This often includes the division's psychologist, social workers, therapists, and counselors, all of whom are in charge of assessing and treating "behavioral kids." Once these individuals have been established in the organizational chart, usually ten to twenty-five staff in any given division, I and/or one other trainer will take this team through a three-day workshop.

Over the course of these intensive three days, we will spend time developing a streamlined referral and assessment process from a trauma-informed, family system approach. We'll spend a considerable time on what compassion fatigue looks like and how to identify it in our staff and ourselves. We will provide a "crisis game plan" manual that we have designed with a number of divisions, providing guideposts for divisions to follow when addressing difficult situations with students and staff. Once these first four stages of the model have been completed in a division or district, that division becomes part of the **Carrington Connections Network** in their respective province or state. They have "back up" from other districts who they can trust speak their same language.

My biggest goal (if I could make anything happen) would be this three-day training of divisional clinical teams becomes the universal standard of school-based mental health care across North America. This simple, standardized three-day training would equip the clinical teams in every division to approach mental health concerns of students and staff in a comprehensive way and from a common place of understanding.

5. Network Certification

If you're part of a division that belongs to the **Carrington Connections Network**, you will have access to support from other divisions when it's required (e.g., the death of a student or staff member, a potential school threat involving a lockdown with police presence, or a significant accident involving the school community). This might look like a case consultation between wellness teams, or a principal to principal phone call when one is navigating their students and staff through a significant loss. The Network is designed with measures in place for each province or state to have exclusive and confidential access to each other's wellness team staff for crisis support.

There's also a yearly one-day conference (in person or virtually) attendance requirement to maintain your **Carrington Connections Network** status. The purpose of a yearly gathering is two-fold: to ensure the integrity of the Network, connecting each district with a contact from other districts before a crisis occurs, and to review the latest trauma-sensitive research and share best practice in assessment and building villages for your hardest students.

A Few Words on Outcome Measures

As this model has progressed, we have relied largely on qualitative data. We have seen a significant decline in overall staff fatigue in a number of the divisions we're working with, as well as an increase in understanding student's stories and needs. We're currently in the development phases of formally measuring the implementation of this model, with a primary focus on staff efficacy. Results will be available soon, so stay tuned.

Last But Not Least, the Jackasses

You're not a Jackass Whisperer for your staff. Don't forget that. Your job isn't to keep everyone happy as you lead them through the trenches.

Let me just take you back to what we talked about with the kids for a minute: You've got to get their hearts first. Connection before direction. The staff who need it the most will be the hardest to give it to, but once you have "followed the lead" for as long as possible (make sure you consult with a trusted colleague on your capacity to follow the lead), there may, in fact, be a take-charge moment. You are the leader, after all. You can't do this alone. I want you to start thinking about, at the very least, how you can (re)connect with other divisions around you. I want you to start thinking about how you're looking after each other.

CHAPTER SEVEN

Game Plan Highlight Reel

Creating a culture of connection among staff becomes integral if we ever hope to connect well with students.

1. It's time we focus much more of our efforts on what we each bring to the table to shift the culture. Relationship knows no hierarchy. We each have a responsibility to lift each other up so we can stay in the game.

2. A whole staff team speaking the "same language" can become the most powerful shift a team can make.

3. Developing a trauma-informed, relationship-focused, standardized training for clinical mental health teams in every

school division in North America was the impetus for the Carrington Connections Network, laid out in this chapter.

4. Linking all divisions trained in this regard within each province and state into a network of support will ensure sustainability when hard things come.

5. This will lead us nicely into our last and final chapter, where we (finally) get to talk about you. And how amazing you are. It's my favorite one. It's where we'll go over how we keep you in the game. Read on and we'll wrap it up.

CHAPTER SEVEN

THE CARRINGTON CONNECTIONS NETWORK FOR EDUCATORS

This little chapter right here is all about "what next?". I think it's always easiest to come up with all of the problems we are facing in the world, but my (our) biggest challenge is to figure out how we respond to them. Not suggestions about what "administrators" need to do, but how do we start to think about this from the inside out? How do we develop a language within a school district that can serve to shift the way it operates, fundamentally, so that everything from pedagogy to parental involvement will reflect relationships—first. End of story. (And PS: If you know a division who might benefit from having me train their mental health team in this model, send them our way!)

1. "Relationship knows no hierarchy" has become the foundation for our approach in every school division we have worked with. Discuss the benefits of having all members of an education system be able to speak the same language. Talk about the barriers that a division or an organization might face as we lead with the "culture first."

2. Kids are kids are kids. This understanding highlighted the necessity to start to network school divisions with each other. Talk about the potential benefits and costs of having access to support from other divisions' mental health teams and administrator supports.

3. Sometimes shifting culture in any team can be a huge challenge. Write down and discuss some of the ways that you can influence the culture in your organization. Hint: These can be little, or they can be huge. A few of my favorites thus far: Meat tray Mondays, a weekly commitment to make a positive call to the tough kids' parents, kindness teams. Any other ideas?

6 STRATEGIES AND STORIES TO KEEP YOU LIT FOR THE WHOLE SCHOOL YEAR

8

THE KIDS ARE THE LEAST OF OUR WORRIES

The final chapter. (insert drum roll here—like booming bass with woofers and tweeters to signify that the answer to the world is about to be revealed. That's how important this chapter is.) First—I can't believe I'm finally here as I write these words—about to wrap up this book. I might be crying a little. It's a dream that I never thought would actually come true—to advocate for educators. Thank you for joining me on this journey. Secondly—this is the most important chapter. Time for the serious shit. This is the one I want you to pay attention to the most. This is the one where we talk about how we look after you.

In the history of the world, we've notoriously looked after the most sacred of our generation. We recognized the wise elders, respected those most talented by rolling out the red carpet, and held in high regard those who led our nations (generally speaking). What about educators? I keep saying this, but I believe it to be true—some of the holiest work on our planet happens within the walls of our schools.

You hold our babes through their most formative years, often for more hours a day than us parents do. If those of you holding our babes on a daily basis are not okay, our kids don't stand a chance.

What Happens if You're Not Okay?

If we're going to build a model for educators that ensures you're "trauma-informed" and have an appreciation for the difference between grief and mourning, what happens if *you* have trauma or grief too? Or, what if when holding and teaching these babies, educators vicariously take on their trauma and grief and take it home? We need to invest in the systems that hold our babies, if our hope is that someday those same babes are going to become part of societal systems to change the world. If our children are held by empty and increasingly disconnected systems, they will create an empty system themselves. You repeat what you don't repair. The time is critical now to do everything we can to stay (re)connected.

Teachers Are Not Okay

Our resources are wearing thin. We started on this quest to decide if teachers these days needed more support, or were they really doing okay? In data from Alberta in 2016, it was reported that one in three teachers and educational assistants and/or their families are prescribed antidepressants or anti-anxiety medication. Within the general population, the average is 1 in 10.[96] The data, both qualitatively and quantitatively, is clear: We're asking those in our education system to hold increasingly complex stories more and more often. This increase in frequency has left many reporting they feel ill-equipped to handle these significant changes in student needs.[97]

And then, everywhere I went, I asked teachers and educators if they are okay. For those with a little more experience under their belts, we asked, "Is your work different these days compared to when you first started teaching or working within the school system?" The responses have varied in every school I've had the privilege to step into, but one theme that continually rises up is that the "difficult" children have always been there. Many educators have explained to me that the "intensity" of having to teach "difficult kids" is not new; however, it is the *frequency* of the difficult stories that appears to be increasing. And here's why that's a problem: When you have one "bad one," or one who completely breaks your heart in a group of twenty kids, you can do many things to support and gain traction for that one student. The other twenty-nine serve largely to fill you up and keep you in the game. When the frequency of the kids who struggle increases, however, our resources tend to wear thin. The research matches what we observe: The frequency is increasing. One in every five students has a plan for self-harm[98]; it won't be long until you're going to feel like you're just not enough.

Thankfully senior leadership has acknowledged that mental health and healthy relationships need to be a national and systems priority. The road map on how to do that has been largely unclear, though, and the default process has been to treat or "fix" the kids. It makes sense that we would try to address what appears to be the problem, especially when kids' self-reports of anxiety and disconnection continue to be alarming. But the kids aren't the ones who we should (solely) be focusing on. Kids these days who struggle the most are often caught in a disconnected system and when we don't look after the people who hold them, everyone suffers.

Compassion Fatigue

That term "compassion fatigue" was first coined in 1992 by Dr. Charles Figley,[99] who described it as a "secondary PTSD" experienced by people in the helping professions. He identified it as a form of burnout and considered it more intense than just simply burning out from too many expectations or demands. Compassion fatigue was meant to identify those of us whose souls get altered by the stories we hold.

Decades later, Dr. Gabor Maté[100] counters this by explaining that although the construct of compassion fatigue is a valid one, the experience of compassion fatigue cannot exist because, as humans, we are wired for compassion. In our human race, you cannot get "fatigued" by what you are wired to do. What happens instead, he says, is when we're triggered by our own trauma, our own stories we have yet to make sense of get stuck, we armor up, and get exhausted by work that used to fuel us.

Think about a time when you worked with a kid who had all of your tolerance and patience, a kid who could do remarkably inappropriate things or hurl hurtful responses, but it somehow didn't bother you. You noticed other colleagues demanded consequences or expulsion and you found yourself trying to protect this student.

Conversely, has there ever been a kid who just got to you so much it surprised you? That you felt exhausted just thinking about him or her? Others had no problem, but there was just something about *that* kid that got to you. Dr. Maté would say it's in those stories (and people) that our own trauma gets triggered. And when we have no safe place, no support to talk about that trauma, no connection to others who might help us, we armor up even more, which makes it harder to deal with the tough stuff. And eventually, the longer we do this work, those stories will pile up in our hearts. And we get tired. We just get tired of caring so damn much. It's time, my friends, even when we must hold the stories that trigger our own trauma, we also figure out how to look after ourselves, first.

"Taking care of yourself doesn't mean 'me first.' It means 'me, too.'"

—L.R. Knost[101]

If you're over the age of eight, the days of putting yourself first have long since passed, my friend. That ship has sailed. Many self-care strategists encourage those of us doing hard things to take care of ourselves first, often with brilliant suggestions like "Take a bubble bath" or "Settle in with a good book." These strategies are obviously for the retired, single, and childless! Here's the thing: If I could find bubbles to put in the bath and actually get in without sitting on Iron Man or Barbie, I would probably get electrocuted checking my email while immersed in the damn tub! And read a book?! Are you kidding me?! I listen to everything now on Audible. While I'm driving. No time for wasting time, I tell you! See, there'll always be an excuse and another demand, particularly if you've no idea how critically important it is to look after "you, too."

We know this to be true: You can't serve from an empty cup. No matter how much you want to help kids, or be a good parent, daughter, grandson, grandparent, partner, human, you will only be at your best if you look after you first. All of us, no matter our race, religion, financial security, or position held in the administrative hierarchy, want to feel we matter and we're making a difference. Relationship and connection know no hierarchy. We all have the power to show each other that every single day.

There is a basic list of things that are critical to consider, like drinking half your body weight in ounces of water every day, getting solid sleep, and moving your body at least 30 minutes a day. Those three things are foolproof and so completely necessary. Making us a priority by looking after our bodies will never be a waste of time. I promise you. Easy enough to do, hard to maintain, but you and I will feel remarkably better when we put the "basics" in our daily routine.

I want to offer you a few additional things to consider, sweet ones (six to be exact). I want you to hang on to these as you navigate your way through another school year. No matter if it's September or June when you're reading these words, I want you to try at least one of these things. Especially if you're not feeling like the hero I know that you are. Deal?

The Six Practices to Keep You Lit for the Whole School Year

These are my go-to practices to keep me in the game. They're the things I have learned from others along the way and have become practices I now cannot function well without. Sometimes I have all six on full speed, and other times I have to check back to the list because I feel empty or overwhelmed. These are in no particular order and I hope you will find them helpful. After all, we need you sweet ones, more than ever, for our kids these days.

1. Bottom Hands Only. The Rest Don't Score.

Who in your world matters most? Whose opinions do you hold the closest? They can be dead or alive, but who in your world do you want to impress the most? Who would you want to make proud? You might never have even met them, but you admire them greatly. I first remember learning about this from two different mentors during two different chapters of my life. Dwayne, a police officer who survived a long career in the force, the death of a child, and stayed happily married to the same woman for forever, once told me he often thought about what his mother would think when he made choices. Every time he made a decision in his marriage or in his career, his aim was to make his mother proud. That stuck with me. The next time was when I was at the Children's Hospital and my mentor Paul, also a man of incredible integrity with beautiful relationships in his life, told me that making his wife proud of him dictated most of his decisions. Those two taught me so much, but I never quite got it until recently.

I have always cared what others think. So much more than I wish I did. Not unlike most, I suppose. It was in graduate school when I first learned about Clance and Imes's[102] imposter phenomenon. It spoke to me. I took much solace. They originally used the term to describe an internal experience of "intellectual phonies" and noted this to be particularly prevalent among high-achieving women. Essentially, it's the name given to those of us who feel that at any moment, people are going to uncover what we believe to be the truth: We're actually frauds and don't belong, we have no business making or stating opinions in our given field, and that we are probably "too big for our britches." I'm telling you, I live in fear of this all the time. I can have 100 comments following a talk that are lovely and glowing, but I will always, always, always focus on the one comment that said I swore too much, was boring, was just there to "make people cry," that I was not inclusive, or that I was offensive. Now, there's a big difference between constructive criticism, which I gladly receive, and the fine line into self-doubt I cross all the time.

Like Dwayne and Paul taught me long ago, it's a select few who you either know or who you admire from afar who can inspire you (likely because of their high moral standards). Can you get a few of those people in your head right now? Remember: dead or alive and you might never have even met them. Write them down, right now. Shoot for five, but there's no magic number. Look at that list carefully. It can change over time, but those are the people right now who I want you to think about every time you need to make big decisions. **The rest don't score**. I mean it.

I'll share my list of who really matters to me. The first is a woman I met only one time. The backstory is that I met her the morning I was to give a keynote at a Canada-wide conference. I was fairly new on the scene and had a number of recent imposter moments leading up to this particular date. This anxiety of mine was fueled in reality, as there had been a lot of discussion leading up to the event about whether I was an appropriate choice to keynote such a prestigious conference. Worries that I might swear too much were expressed. There was a *lot* of discussion about the swearing. And concerns that I was too bold. And not an educator. Apparently, phone calls had been made to organizers, yet no one had shared their concerns with me directly—yet. I thought all concerns had been previously addressed; however, shortly before I was to take the stage for the keynote, I was given a warning about how to conduct myself. I was a wreck inside as a result. I thought about just leaving. Packing it all in. I should have been a barista. Who did I think I was anyway? And this colloquial style of mine—maybe it did have to go? I often swear when I talk about important things. Even on stage. But I do so with a purpose. Primarily because I think there are a few words in our respective languages that demand attention (not necessarily respect), and in my world, I'm often talking about a lot of things that require immediate attention and have been overlooked for decades. I had always justified in my head that being me and bringing my message with purpose and truth is how it should be. But maybe I was wrong? Maybe I needed to conform to a mold if I ever hoped that people would listen? (In fact, I can attest to the multiple, relentless conversations we had about this very topic before we could ever dream of going to print for this book. Even my husband and I had many discussions about this. I'd come home with a broken heart after trying to defend my style. He would wonder, in his protective way, if I should alter things. I told him the successful people I'd admired for years swore on stage all the time. Like Brené Brown, or Tony Robbins. Aaron was quick to point out I was not quite on par with Tony, at this point in my life anyway. Tony, he gently reminded me, had a jet. And 10 million followers. Fuck that.)

But, back to being a fish out of water at the conference. Back to meeting *her*. As I was contemplating my escape route moments before taking to the stage, she approached me at the buffet table. A young, beautiful woman, maybe in her mid-thirties. She apologized for approaching me and said she'd heard me speak once before and was so excited to be here today to hear me again. We chatted briefly about why she was at this conference for educators, when she explained that she was not a teacher—but her husband was. I asked her where he taught now, and she told me it was "a long story." When I said, "Tell me more," my heart broke as she explained that her husband had been killed in a car accident two years earlier along with their 10-month-old daughter. She and her two sons had also been in the vehicle and had survived. Every single day she was struggling to live well for them and to serve her husband and her daughter's legacy. She told me it was when she heard me speak, reminding her she was wired to do hard things, that she believed it was going to be okay. She told me her favorite parts were that I was "real" and most importantly (at least how I remember it anyway) was that I swore. She told me that since that day, she was able to look at the hardest time in her life and still be able to smile sometimes. She said to me, "Keep doing what you're doing. It's changing people. And promise me you'll never dull your light." And that was the day she became one of my five. I take her with me to every talk I ever give. I sent her a message months later, telling her about the impact she had on me. I also wanted her to know that, in more ways than she could imagine, her husband and her daughter's legacy had impacted many.

My other four? My brother always comes with me. We've been through a lot, he and I. He's wise beyond his years and one of the few people who, when he speaks, I listen. Growing up, he was often mortified by my loudness and now, he will just sit back and shake his head. When he's proud of me, I know I am doing something right.

Third is my Grandpa Jack. He died ten years ago, before he got to see me get married or have children. I don't think, however, there has been a human being on this planet who was prouder of me. He would often introduce me to his coffee buddies as "Dr. Jody." I asked him once if he had any idea what kind of doctor I was, and he said, "Nope and it doesn't matter."

I also need someone on my list who keeps me in the game when the mother of all guilt comes calling: Am I being a good mom? I tell you, it's my biggest battle. How is it that we can smash traditional gender roles and still be a mama who bakes cookies every day when our kids get home from school? I was inspired by a woman who I'd only known for a year before she lost her battle to cancer. She's my number four. She was an incredible mom and a kind soul. I knew she had huge hopes and dreams for her son and daughter, and I cannot imagine what it must have been like knowing she would not be here to watch those dreams get realized. I take Tara with me often. When I question whether I am serving my own children well, I think of her. I know that she would give anything to say to her babies, "Watch mama change the world," while I remind you, as often as I'm able, that I'm crazy about you. I want our children to know a world where there are no male and female leaders—just leaders. And I want our children to grow up in a world where they know, without a doubt, that women are the CEOs of companies *and* they have incredible children who know they're loved. She is my bottom hand on the days when I need it the most and I do my very best to live well for the both of us.

My husband Aaron (sometimes I take him off the list when it comes to the swearing part), and my lucky three—my three best friends—Tannis, Leigha, and Rhea are always my ride-or-dies. They each light me up like sunshine. I want to be close to them because they are like "home" to me. My mom has always been my safe place to land, a woman of strength and integrity. My dad has inspired me to be nothing less than phenomenal and to dream big. There are a select few others who travel with me from time to time when I need to make a decision about what I stand for in this life. These ones. They are who I write to, who I speak to, who I try and remember to parent to, they are who I think about when Aaron and I have a fight. Find your four or five, my loves. In those big moments, only their opinions matter. **The rest don't score.**

2. Choose Joy

It's ridiculous to me that we have to talk about joy as a conscious choice. Like, on the surface, doesn't it make sense that any one of us would choose joy over anything else, if we had the choice? But as Brené Brown discovered in her research on vulnerability and shame, joy is the most vulnerable emotion on the planet.

Just think about that for a moment. When do you feel the freest? When people who are struggling come to me, no matter the reason, one of the things I like to ask is when was the last time they belly laughed with their babes. Or danced in their kitchen with their partner? Or noticed the light-up in someone's eyes that was intended just for them? Like the outstretched arms of a child running to meet you. Like the flying embraces you witness at airport reunions. Like getting that good news you know, without a doubt, you deserve. That feeling underneath it all.

For many of us, this emotion, remarkably, triggers fear. Many generations before us have been taught if things are going too well, that must mean something bad is going to happen. We like to think if we prepare for the worst, we will be ready for it when it comes. But here's the deal: Although many believe we can experience two emotions at the same time, rarely can we actually experience both emotions with the same intensity. One usually wins. So, while you are busy preparing for the worst (so you'll be ready when the hypothetical situation hypothetically happens), what are you missing? That's right. You're missing the joy. I promise you, any parent who received "that phone call" or that "knock on the door" would say no amount of preparation on this planet could have readied them for what it was like to receive that news. What I do know, however, is the more we prepare for it, the more time we're stealing away from what we do have in the moment with those we love.

Leaning in to joy, for me, means slowing down long enough to notice the little things. And believe me, they're everywhere. Putting yourself on a mission, every day, to seek the little things, will often bring them to the light. It must be a conscious effort. We have to practice it. Otherwise, our default will be to dress-rehearse tragedy. Here's the other cool thing: When you notice those little things and are so bold as to point them out to others, you bring joy to others (and yourself). It's the biggest secret superpower we all possess. It's free and it's infinite.

Just Notice: Joy is Everywhere

Here's a little story I have shared many times. I think of this woman often. I pulled up to a traffic light one sunny afternoon in my old college town. I was in my head, prepping for the training I was about to step into that day (and reliving my glory days of 1993 when I was walking these streets at 2:00 a.m. after an evening of drinking and dancing at Billy Bob's). Then the woman in the vehicle behind me caught my attention. She was a mama, I guessed, in a beat-up old minivan. And she was dancing in the driver's seat as she was sitting, waiting for the light. I watched in my rear-view mirror as she rocked out, with a head flip for effect. I laughed out loud as I watched the little person in the front passenger seat beside her—about 13 years old—mortified. If he could have crawled into the vents, he would have. I grabbed my colleague's arm in the seat beside me and said, "Watch this mama!" The child in the front seat of her van was wearing a helmet, so he may have had a developmental delay, and was losing his mind that his mama (I assumed) was being ridiculous. As we stared in awe at her in our rear-view mirror, the light turned green and we didn't notice. People were honking, and we hurried to turn the corner. I let this mama in her minivan (and her dance moves) pass me, and then I followed her. My colleague said, "Where are you going? Training is left, not right." I said, "I know. I just have to follow that mama and tell her she's amazing." "Right *now*?!" my colleague asked. "Yes, right now."

A few moments later I pulled into her driveway (thankfully she wasn't headed to Winnipeg!), and as she parked, I got out and tapped on her window. She rolled it down hesitantly and I said, "I'm so sorry to bother you, I was just stopped at the traffic light ahead of you back there and I noticed your sweet dance moves." She said, cautiously, "Okay. . ." I proceeded with, "I just wanted to tell you that I don't know who this little man is here beside you, but I think you're amazing and I think he's pretty lucky to have you." And you know what she said to me? After a deep breath, and a pause, she said, "Thank you. I needed that." I walked back to my vehicle, saying, "Have a great day," and as I got back into my car, we watched as she carried this boy, cradled in her arms, into the house; he was immobile. He couldn't walk. See—this mama. She's amazing. She was bringing joy to her sweet babe in that moment and she was dancing for nobody. She brought me so much joy in that single moment, and I needed her to know that. As moms, dads, teachers, caregivers, we need do that every day—to dance for nobody. But when somebody notices, isn't that the most amazing thing? When people notice, it can so often fill you to the core. Do you think this mama was back in the game? Even if just for a few moments. It cost me nothing. I'm telling you, we have the capacity to change the trajectory of this broken world simply by (re)connecting. Lean in to moments of joy that are everywhere, just waiting to be noticed. Don't ever forget your power.

Now how does one stay in the moment? If joy is such a fantastic choice, many ask me, then how do I friggin' do it? Particularly when I'm overwhelmed and "spinning"? How do I slow down long enough to notice the moments in other people? Here's the deal. Like anything you want to get good at, it takes practice.

3. Gratitude and Intention

Gratitude is a practice for a reason. It's like yoga, your faith, or taking the perfect wrist shot from the point. You can want it all day long but watching it on YouTube or reading about it doesn't make it something you will get good at doing. You must practice it. Staying longer in moments of joy becomes easier to do when we practice gratitude.

Now see, I've read so much about gratitude. Particularly gratitude journals. It's cognitive-behavioral therapy 101. Change your thoughts and it'll change your feelings. And you should really write it down. There are reams of data that say our brains process much more beautifully when we write. It slows us down enough to examine our thoughts and reconnect to our stories. I often recommend journaling to my clients. I, myself, am not a big fan though. Going through my old hope chest that my mother so lovingly kept (I'm not sure exactly what we were hoping for when it was stuffed with my old glasses and doilies I got for my ninth grade grad, but I digress), I found diary entries from my teen years, love notes from boys, and me trying to make sense of broken hearts. It all freaks me out. I can't even read my poems out loud. I hurt for that girl. I know she will figure it all out eventually, but those years were not pretty. And these days, I've always worried about what might happen to my words if I suddenly died and someone found them.

To practice gratitude, the options are to send yourself emails to a secret email address that only you have the password to or writing down three things every morning. I do that—what I'm thankful for. Let's be honest, the actual writing takes place a couple times a week, when I remember, when I have a pen. I do try my hardest, however, to get in my head three things I'm thankful for every single morning. And I have a couple of rules that govern this little practice. Don't let the rules throw you off—you can stop right here if this is already too much for you. Every day the three things you choose have to be different than the day before. I had to add this rule, because I would just do my standard three without much connection: kids, house, and husband every morning, without much thought, because I said I would. The second thing I try to remember to do before I even set feet on the floor is to *not* reach for my phone. That friggin' phone is where I throw myself off every morning—sinking myself into the social media abyss before settling into my own soul (another extremely helpful tip is to charge your phones outside of the bedroom).

When coming up with your gratitude three, think of the things going on right, right now. Your safe havens, your looking-forward-tos. And notice—just notice—what happens to your body when you do. You can try it right now. If you think about the three things you're truly thankful for, what happens to your breathing? To your shoulders? Maybe to the tension in your face. Stopping for a moment to slow down the crazy can change everything. When you do that, you come back to yourself. Ever so slightly. And that is where your best version of yourself resides. And that, my friend, is what we need a little more of in this world. Anxiety or depression cannot live in a relaxed body. Slow it down as many times a day as you can muster. It's magic.

Intentions are a whole other ball game. What is an intention anyway? Is it a prayer without really having to ask someone for it? Who is in charge of intentions? And who do I think I am, setting intentions? What happened to trusting the universe? Here's the deal. I don't know (or care) if there's scientific proof behind this, because I know it works for me. Setting an intention to focus more on something or someone, to bring awareness to an emotion or a connection with someone or something, will bring that into focus. A clear distinction is seeking an intention from a place of contentment rather than arising from a sense of desperation or need. In the morning or before you fall asleep (without phone in hand), make some space for an intention. Just like gratitude, write them down if you can. At the very least, get them in your head. Here are some of my favorites:

- Today, I intend to understand first, and then seek to be understood.
- Today, I intend to lead by example.

- Tomorrow, when I wake up, I intend to be open to success and abundance.
- Today, my intention is to open my heart to others in service, to be kind, especially to the ones who need it the most.

If we're thinking gratitude and intention, sinking in to the stories and people who have taught me the most often bring me to a place a thankfulness. Like this mama, for example.

Her name is Kelly. I had just started my private practice and was doing some consulting with a local agency. There was a request to see a mama who had been through the system and was one step away from losing her kid. They explained that my meeting her was the one last shot to see if I could convince her of the changes necessary for her to keep her kid. I was reluctant with the tall task at hand but agreed to just one session. No pressure.

At the time, Kelly was a large woman. She came in wearing stretchy pants and a tank top. She walked through the door with the stance of a fighter. Elbows out. And tattoos everywhere. Hair pulled back in a loose ponytail, a hint of a purple dye (her favorite color) outlining the fringe. She came up to the counter, where I was waiting for her, and she spit out these words: "I'm here to meet Julie or Jessie or Judy or something. I was told to come here." (This is always a good opener for a therapist. No small feat.) Connection before direction, right? So, I said, "Hey. I'm Jody. Are you Kelly?" She replied, "Yeah."

It was 9:30 a.m. My next question was, "Do you want a root beer?" She said, "Fuck, ya." And we were connected every Monday for the next two years. I met with her parents, with her boyfriend, and with her sweet boy (sometimes chasing him down the block when he told me to "Fuck off" and "Stop making my mom cry").

One of my biggest accomplishments with that sweet mama, who loved her boy dearly, was shifting her belief in herself. I didn't do that with any fancy therapy. Turns out there is no therapy for that. I found out what she loved, and then I did too. She collected butterflies. She showed me pictures of the wall in her home of all the butterfly art she'd collected, proudly displayed. I found her butterflies a few times when I was out of town. The other thing I noticed about this woman was that she was smart. Really smart. At 33 years old, she didn't drive, because she didn't believe she could pass the Learners Driving Test. We had study cards and every week we would go through questions, piling the ones she crushed on one side and throwing the ones she didn't yet know on the other. And we went through them again. And again. And again. Until I was sure she could coach anyone in the world how to write the damn test. Finally, I convinced her, during a session, that it was time. And we walked across the back alley from my office to the registry office (the beauty of living in a small town).

I don't know about your town, but the registry employees here take their job very seriously. There will be no loud talking, there will be waiting your turn, and you better have all your documents in order. They mean business. So as Kelly and I approached the counter, we worked hard to stay kind in the clipped manner with which we were greeted. As she sat down in the waiting room behind a little cubical to write this test, I sat five feet away. And prayed. I have to tell you, I don't remember ever praying that hard (except when my baby son was in the NICU). I wanted this mama to win so badly. I knew how hard she'd worked. And I knew she was capable.

When she slid her chair back in what felt like way too little time, she walked over to me in the same stance she used when we first met. Her face stoic. I searched her eyes for the answer, already preparing all of the soothing responses I might need to pull out. And then she said, "I FUCKING PASSED!" I screamed! And I remember us hugging and jumping, with a lot of boob bouncing in the small waiting room, while our very respectable registry ladies watched with disapproval. I've never before not cared what others thought so much in my life.

Today, this mama and I still light up when we see each other. Her boy continues to struggle, but he's in school. Kelly got engaged to a sweet man and they moved into an apartment with more room. Just last month she sent me a picture of their wedding day, with a note that read:

> *Good morning, Jody. I wanted to share a wonderful day with you that I thought would never happen for me 'cause I didn't think I was worth it. Thank you for showing me that I was. [Name] and I got married on Saturday. Thank you again, Jody.*

I will save this message always. This mama is amazing.

I know you have stories just like this one about moms and dads you've met and babies who found their spark, all because of you. That's where I want you to go when the haters come. And they will. They always do. Usually because they're hurting even more than you. And they've lost their gratitude.

4. Practicing the F-Word

The F-word, sweet ones, is not what you might think (or hope); it's about forgiveness. It made "the list" of the top six things I want you to keep in your back pocket because it's one of the most important things you can do to keep you in the game.

Many people think of forgiveness as letting go or moving on, but as it turns out, it's not that easy. There's more to it than that, as many, like Dr. Robert Enright,[103] a researcher on forgiveness, has come to understand. He writes, true forgiveness goes a step further than just "forgive and forget." True forgiveness, the kind that sets you free, involves the step of offering something positive—empathy, compassion, understanding—toward the person who hurt you. It's this element that takes this whole forgiveness thing to a whole new level. It doesn't suffice, turns out, to say, "Oh, I forgive them all right.

And I hope they die a slow painful death." That doesn't have the same vibe as, "It has taken me a long time, but I do forgive him. It was a difficult time for both of us. I wish him happiness."

I think it's important to clarify that my suggestion doesn't mean condoning or letting the person who wronged you off the hook. Forgiveness isn't the same as justice, nor does it require reconciliation.[104] A former victim of abuse should not reconcile with an abuser who remains potentially dangerous, for example. But the victim can still come to a place of empathy and understanding in order to heal and move forward.

> *"Whether I forgive or don't forgive isn't going to affect whether justice is done. Forgiveness happens inside my skin."*
>
> —Everett L. Worthington

Research has shown that forgiveness is linked to positive mental health outcomes such as reduced anxiety, a reduction in depression and major psychiatric disorders, fewer physical health symptoms, and lower mortality rates. In fact, Worthington and Williams wrote a whole book about the benefits of forgiveness and repair, noting the many physical and psychological benefits.[105]

Even for the little things, forgiveness and repair are hard to do. Like the time I flew home from Los Angeles not long ago, after spending a few days planning for the years ahead. It was an exciting time. Aaron had also just finished an intense few days schmoozing in his world of cows and agriculture, so I was pleased we would get 10:00-11:30 p.m. all to ourselves, in a truck, driving home from the airport. Somewhere between the luggage collection and me having to wait ten minutes for him to get from the cell phone lot, I got super annoyed. First, my phone wouldn't let a call out—and he wasn't waiting there as I had expected. Seriously? I just wanted to get home to my babies. He was probably sleeping. Come *on*! As the minutes (and they were just literally about four minutes) ticked by, I got really friggin' annoyed. When he pulled up to the curb, I opened the back door of his truck to lift my own suitcase in (because apparently chivalry is dead). I saw him look at me with a smile and say, "Hi, honey!" My response (and I even cringe when I write this) was, "What were you doing? I've been here for like twenty minutes." It's a bit foggy, but I think I followed this with the F-word—but I swear I said that before I opened the passenger door. I swear.

When I got in the truck, which smelled like feedlot (another impressive factor), he was clearly not cool with my lack of gratitude. "Well, that's a fine welcome. Maybe a 'hello, honey' would be nice?" And then, you know what I said? "Okay. Dude. I don't have time for a lecture right now. I'm tired. You were late. And I just want to get home." He said, in a measured (and slightly condescending tone, I might add), "I. Had. To. Drive. Here. From. The. Cell. Phone. Lot." And then radio silence. Not a question about how things had gone. Not a further attempt to soften the situation. Nothing. So, then you know what I thought: "Oh you big friggin' baby. Come *on*!" (in my head only, thankfully).

See, I knew what I had to do there. I knew I needed to repair it. I know it would work. I know he needs it. And I know it wouldn't be hard. But I didn't want to do it. I did attempt a "soft" repair that sounded like this: "Did you get your hair cut?" He nods, barely noticeable, and I say, "It looks good." He says, "Thanks," barely audible. Well—there you have it folks. I tried. I tried to be nice. What more do you want from me? I'm tired, I'm working my ass off for our family, and now you're going to act like you're two years old because I wasn't kind in my greeting? Fine. Then I'll just look at my phone. Maybe text someone who cares. Turns out I'm going to be just fine in this world. I could raise three kids by myself. Why do people stay in relationships anyway? Like seriously.

So, now, with that beautiful mantra to guide my way home, we didn't speak. We got back to the house, he (very chivalrously) grabbed my suitcase—his soft attempt at repair, I would imagine—and I stormed in the house ahead of him. The babes were in bed, so we went to bed too, me pulling the covers on my side tight (just in case he wasn't clear I was not happy with him). Again, I knew what needed to be done, but I couldn't do it. It would be easy. An apology. But instead I fell asleep and so did he. And we woke up the next morning still in a cone of silence. The kids offered a nice distraction, but he was doing nothing to help get them through their morning routine. Normally, he would be up getting breakfast for them, but now he was still lying in bed, scrolling through his phone, obviously just to piss me off. As words like "lazy" and "disrespectful" floated in my head, I decided enough was enough. He was leaving later that day and would be gone on the road again for a few days and I knew it was now or never. So, I beckoned him to the bathroom.

When I looked at him in the eyes, I tried not to smile as I said, "I'm so sorry. I just wasted a whole evening with you. I shouldn't have snapped at you." He said, "Thanks." I waited for an apology too, but it didn't come. I could feel the "but, you could have..." bubble up in my throat and it took everything, I mean everything, not to say those words. I wanted to suggest maybe next time he might roll with it a little easier, or like maybe tell me to have a drink on the plane before every arrival home, from here on in, or to use some of that dry humor of his that I love. But alas, I will save that for another day.

In her most recent book, *Why Won't You Apologize*,[106] Harriet Lerner, one of the gems in my world, talks about how we're losing the art of apology and repair. To truly repair a relationship, it's best done face to face. And it's not easy. It's much more comfortable to not talk about it and to avoid conflict or check your phone. And an apology that works does not contain the word "but." When you say "but" after an apology, you erase the apology. And an apology also does not sound like this: "I'm sorry you feel that way" or "I'm sorry you're so sensitive." This becomes a shaming response. It's like saying, "If you weren't such a baby, we wouldn't be here."

A true apology sounds like this: "I'm sorry." End of story. You do it for you as much as you do it for them. That F-word and repair are powerful things, my friend. Use them often to heal and care for yourself.

5. Collective Effervescence

This strategy made the list because I wanted something to remind you about the importance of staying connected with your team. After all, we're wired to do hard things, but we do those things so much easier when we remember we're wired for connection. The power of this concept is so simple, yet often difficult to execute. Collective effervescence[107] was introduced by a guy named Émile Durkheim in the early 1900s (again, note another reference to a dead guy). He proposed that a community or society may at times come together. The result, he wrote, is a "collective effervescence" that creates excitement and commitment, and unifies a group or team to become a force as one. This concept is not new, but we forget it so often, particularly as the school year wears on and the frequency of dysregulated babies become more prominent. Imagine what it would look like in our schools (and communities) if we created more collective effervescence?

Here's how it makes sense for me: Imagine for a second that you're in downtown Toronto (or any big city) in the early evening, and you see a kid with dreads and a backpack just hanging out. What is the probability that you would approach this kid and ask him if he'd like to join you for dinner? Not likely, right? Now imagine you're in Europe, in a place where your primary language is not the same as everyone else's, and you've had very little connection to others for days. As you hike into town, you see a kid with dreads and a backpack just hanging out. Then you notice a Canadian flag on his backpack. Would you approach this kid? It's more likely now, isn't it? I might say, "Hey! Canada!? Me too!" And then we would fall into asking where each other is from and if they know a Mike who lived in Toronto.

See, when we can find things that bind us together, we are more likely to want to connect and stay connected. This plays out in every sports arena across the world. If you love a team, and you're there cheering exuberantly for that team, you might be wearing the team jersey. You might have painted your face, or worn a carved-out watermelon on your head because that's what die-hard fans do, right? When you see others who are clearly for "your team," you'll high-five them, hoot and holler. None of these things you would do with other people on the street if you didn't know they were also cheering for your team. It's a collective bringing together for one belief (a team) that fills us with pride and commitment and loyalty.

See, "People are hard to hate close up: We're more alike than we are different."[108] There are others who have said these words before. I love them. Since the first time I read those words, it has changed the way I think about people, colleagues, and even my husband. It's not unlike everything we've been talking about for the past six chapters: When we get hurt our first instinct is to pull away and put up a wall. It makes sense that we wouldn't run to the fire, especially if we've been burned before. And this is especially true when things are fundamentally different from us. It's so much easier to assume that our differences mean we're right and they're wrong. The dismissiveness becomes easy. But what becomes more powerful is moving **into** the people who are on your team, who are also doing this holy work.

Just like with kids, the hardest ones to give it to are the ones who need it the most. Think about your staff team. Think about the ones who right now don't seem to fit in or have a purpose to their job. They rarely participate and when there, they seem to be in it for only a paycheck. What might be going on with them? How do we create that sense of "we are in this together"? Could it be possible that the most significant impact you can have at work isn't with the kids you teach every day, but the people who walk alongside you doing this hard and holy work? It's empathy—suspending judgement for just a moment and stepping into another's shoes—that will always, always get you there the quickest.

6. Lean In. We Need You.

Number six is last, but certainly not least. The whole leaning in concept is a phrase that caught my heart when I first read Sheryl Sandberg's book with the same title, *Lean In: Women, Work, and the Will to Lead.*[109] She wrote it before the sudden death of her husband, and it encourages women to "lean in" at the table of corporate America and have our voices be heard. She wrote, in *Option B: Facing Adversity, Building Resilience, and Finding Joy,*[110] that she overlooked many things and didn't consider what it might be like for single mothers, or women who didn't want to necessarily lean in. I remember that lesson well. I had just expanded my company to my very first employee, who I still, to this day, call My Marti. I officially met Marti in a cold skating rink at 8:00 a.m. one Saturday morning, when we were sharing time-clock duties for our respective sons' hockey team. I showed up, pleased I was dressed (only to discover my bra wasn't even hooked up) and hoping my son was somewhere on the ice. Marti, who'd prepared coffees in take-away mugs and printed out the score clock instructions after watching a YouTube video, was excited to start the day. As we fumbled our way through the game, me yelling out of the little referee hole (that's apparently frowned upon), I told Marti I needed a little of her organization in my life. She told me that before her three children, she had worked in the corporate world as an assistant and would love to do that work again. BAM. Ever since that day, I have been madly dedicated to this girl who has single-handedly gotten me more organized than I could ever have dreamed possible.

One of the first events Marti and I attended together was a women and leadership conference. I was so excited to talk about women who could take over the world and dream about how we could do amazing things by leaning in at the big table to have our voices heard. And then Marti said something that I will never forget: "But, I don't want to lean in at the big table. I want you to lean in, and I want to be in your corner when you do it, but my lean in will be from the back row. Is that cool?" What?! It was the first time in my life that it had occurred to me that leaning in could look very different for everyone. You might be thinking, WTF, Jody? But I can tell you, I often tell that story about bringing your best self to work every day. Show up as authentically as possible, every damn day, and you will create your own kind of magic. I'll say it again for the people in the back: **Sit with the winners. The conversation is different**. Marti and I work so well together because she's good at everything I'm not (other than keeping plants alive . . . we both suck at that). True diversity on a successful team is important and so is staying true to your vision. Don't get derailed by anything else.

So, here's the deal, whether you're leaning in from the big table, front row, with a gavel, or you're in the second row, giving it all you've got with a whisper: All we need is you and your true self. This is not the time to be humble, my sweet ones. I'm going to need you to get uncomfortable. To lean in to your true power for the lives you influence—and have influenced. I want you to think about your successes and remember them. I want you to make a list of the kids who maybe, just maybe, you changed as you supported them. Those babies may not be able to say thank you—but think about the ones who you know in your heart you helped believe in themselves. Get them in your head right now. That's where I want you to spend some time. I promise you, if you have been in this business for more than six months, you have changed more lives than you can ever imagine. I want you to know it and believe it.

This is hard for me to sit with sometimes, too. I wonder if I've really had an impact. When I start to think about all the stories of the people I've been privileged to know, it sometimes takes my breath away, and then it re-lights my fire. But sometimes I have to think really hard. Sometimes you may never know. Hang on to the ones you do. Keep the notes and the cards. Keep those stories close. Write it down when a student comes back to remind you of your influence. Brag about it in the staff rooms. Share those good ones.

I'm going to wrap it up with one of my best. The one family (and there have been many who have changed me) who I bring into my heart on the days I wonder why I do this work.

It all starts with three babes, ages 9, 7, and 5—two boys and a girl who I'll call Derek, Hannah, and Cohen. These three babes were apprehended by Child and Family Services (CFS) after a number of unsuccessful attempts to prepare biological Mom and Dad to be full time caregivers. These three had witnessed and experienced significant trauma in their short lives, including being a part of domestic violence situations and experiencing significant neglect. Shortly following apprehension, a young couple—Ryan and Beth, we will call them—noticed the three children who had recently joined a foster family in their community. After some contemplation, the couple approached CFS to determine if they would be a fit to first care for and potentially adopt these three babes. In the CFS world, it's always the hope to keep siblings together; however, due to limited placements and lack of potential adoptive homes for older children, especially in a sibling group of three, the situation to keep them all together with a potential adoption was unheard of and truly remarkable.

In reviewing their history, I noted that during the initial year while the three siblings adjusted to their new caregivers, their trauma stories caught up with them. Their lack of "hands on the circle" to help them with their emotional regulation skills had left them all functioning like little ones when they became distressed. Derek, the oldest boy, had significant struggles regulating, would kick and scream when things didn't make sense, would throw things, and often requested to return to his very dysfunctional biological parents, hurling statements like, "You will never be my parents. I will never love you." The middle child, Hannah, was quiet and anxious. She caused very little trouble but would often present with somatic complaints like tummy troubles, difficulty sleeping, and school avoidance. The littlest one, Cohen, struggled the most, having difficulty paying attention, and would threaten to run away, hoard food in his bedroom, and steal items from around the house.

First-time parents Ryan and Beth struggled significantly to make sense of their children's behavior. They worked very hard to earn their affection and were crushed when it wasn't received well or rejected by the children. Although CFS offered support, they listened when parents wondered many times if they didn't have what the children needed. After a number of months of continued struggles and violence, the parents approached CFS and asked that the children be placed back into care. CFS, of course, responded to this request. At the time of my involvement, these foster-potentially-adoptive parents had spent 18 months with the children living in their home. They had fallen in love with all three of them but were worried they would not be able to give them what they needed. CFS brought the children back into care, placed them again with another foster family who were amazingly able to take all three, and there was to be no contact between the children and Ryan and Beth.

As you can imagine, Ryan and Beth were crushed. They missed the children and felt horribly for "failing" them. Later, they decided they could no longer even stay in the community where they parented the children, as their hearts were broken. Ryan took a job transfer and they moved a few hours away. The children were kept together and placed in a foster home in a community outside of where they had been living, meaning they also had to change schools and adjust to new caregivers and siblings.

I became involved after a request to consult on this case when a Permanent Guardianship Order was granted. This meant that the biological parents had now been deemed by the court as unable to care for their children and wouldn't be permitted to have contact with them, for their own safety, until the children could make that decision for themselves. The referral question for the consult included insights on how to help the children say goodbye to their biological parents. In the beginning, I knew nothing about the failed foster-to-adopt attempt with Ryan and Beth.

In reviewing their case, I wondered if there had been someone in the lives of the children who could help them walk through this difficult decision to say a final goodbye to their biological mom and dad. Who could hold their hand when they were told they would no longer be allowed visits with biological mom and dad? That's when I was told about Ryan and Beth, and the role they had played in the lives of the children. I wondered where they were now, and it broke my heart to learn that there had been no follow-up with this family or contact regarding how the children they raised for nearly two years were doing. I asked if I and a supervisor from the youth agency that contracted me could meet with Ryan and Beth, if we could drive to see them. I asked if there was still an opportunity for them to maintain some relationship with the children and to help them make sense of their trauma responses and rejections. Thankfully, I was granted that opportunity and worked alongside a community service provider named Dixie. She and I had not met prior to this file, and I can tell you, to this day, she has become one of my dearest friends.

On our drive to meet Ryan and Beth for the first time (a four-hour trek), Dixie and I talked about attachment, and trauma, and lid flipping—much of what you've read about so far in this book. We agreed we would take it slow with Ryan and Beth, giving them an update on the children before gauging their willingness to be involved again. Both Ryan and Beth were open to, but not overly receptive to, our meeting. When they invited us into their home, they shared with us that they had not seen the children for over a year, and they had been granted only one visit. They also explained that they were surprised by a pregnancy of their own and they introduced us to their three-month-old son! They explained that they poured their energy into him in an effort to cope, but they thought about the children often. They explained that their impression was that they had let CFS down for "giving back" the children and discussed how the decision had been so difficult and painful. We reviewed where the children were at and their memories of their time with Ryan and Beth. The couple were moved to tears to learn the children thought of them so fondly, even after being out of their lives for so long. We talked about how confusing this can be when children have trauma histories and how rejection can often be the only thing that they have to keep themselves safe. We wondered if they'd be open to visits again, at the very least to demonstrate to these babes that sometimes, no matter what, people don't give up. Beth and Ryan were cautious, but so wonderfully back in the game.

To make a long (beautiful) story short, after many slow visits, trauma talks, and support, this sweet couple asked these three babes if they'd like to live with them forever. We celebrated with a cake. And balloons. And here's the cool part: Mama Beth sends us a photo every year on their adoption anniversary. These three children warm me to the core. And, oh yeah, Beth and Ryan got pregnant one more time. You know what they named their sweet baby girl? Dixie.

We are game-changers, sweet ones. We are called to do the work of hanging on to kids and shaping them into amazing souls. You get babies just like this every day. Don't ever forget your power.

Bringing It All Home

Well, ladies and gentlemen, there you have it: A whole collection of words I hope inspire you, based largely on the stories of people who have inspired me. We're the carriers of stories who, if we pay close enough attention, are there to guide us in our work and end up teaching *us* the lessons in our love, and in our lives.

You, simply by the profession you chose, will come with many marks on your hearts. Use them as guideposts in your work forward. Know there is never an "endgame" to teaching "kids these days." There will always be a new crop ready for your wisdom, your insights, your hands on the circle. I'll say it again (and for the rest of my career): What you do is holy work. You are wired to do this. And with all my heart I know this to be true: You are exactly where you need to be.

In these last few words with me, I want you to think about what you want your legacy to be? The highest math grades across your district? Or getting a kid to walk across the graduation stage after being in juvie for most of ninth grade? I'll take you back to the beginning, where the journey of this book started with you and me: to ask yourself, what is your critical purpose? Is it possible that your best work is ahead of you? That your reach to those babes and families who need it the most has not even begun? Look out, planet. Here you come!

CHAPTER EIGHT

Game Plan Highlight Reel

You, sweet educator, must become our first priority. If you're not okay, our kids don't stand a chance.

1. Compassion fatigue is a term coined for those of us who experience the emotional sequelae from working in the helping professions and holding difficult stories.

2. Included in this chapter is a playbook of strategies for you to "stay lit" the whole school year. Pick any one, any time, to help keep you in the game and be the best you've ever been in your career.

3. The most important work we can do is to create teams who are connected to each other so that when we each stumble (and we will), we have a safe place to make sense of it all and get back in the game.

4. By virtue of the profession you chose, you have the capacity to change the trajectory of a life, every single day. You, dear one, are amazing.

The Kids Are the Least of Our Worries

This last little chapter was bittersweet for me. I wanted to leave the most powerful chapter for the end, to be the one that lifted souls and kept those of you doing holy work in the game. The goal, sweet ones, is to look after you. Just a little—or a lot. Nothing in this chapter will steer you wrong. It is a practice, not an endgame. Keeping you in the game means we have to focus on it as often as we can. We need *you*, amazing one.

1. What does "compassion fatigue" mean to you? Do you see it in the people around you? Why, do you think, are some of your colleagues more affected than others?

2. Write down your "bottom hands." Remember, not the people you're thankful for, per se, but the ones whose opinions matter the most to you. The ones you want to show up for. The ones you want to make proud. Share about at least one of your bottom hands and how you got so lucky to be influenced by them.

3. This whole idea of practicing gratitude and joy is often talked about these days, but putting it into action seems to be more of a challenge, and indeed a *daily* practice. Stop for a moment and write down or discuss the three things, right here and right now, that you're most grateful for. Try to get creative, and search for the least obvious things, not "just" kids, family, job, but the ones that take a little effort. Why did they come into your head today, do you think?

MY SEND-OFF

From the bottom of my heart to yours, to each and every single one of you who hold the young souls on this planet just like my three babies every day, in whatever capacity, **thank you**. I am in awe of you. I am humbled by you. And I am so, so grateful for you. You change the world. I hope my words inspire you to continue in your holy work.

Thank you for being with me on this journey. For reading these words. For believing and spreading this message of (re)connection. Share them with your administrators, your teacher friends, your mama, your second uncle, twice removed. Kids these days just need you; they need us. One light-up at a time. Bottom hands only, my friends. The rest don't score.

I'm your biggest fan and I will continue to work, for the rest of my days, to advocate for you. Shine on today and every day, sweet one. Whatever you have is enough. xo

ENDNOTES

Chapter 1: (Re)Connecting Back to the Beginning

1   To learn more about Simon Sinek, check out his
website: https://startwithwhy.com/

2   Alice Walker won the Pulitzer Prize in Literature for her book *The Color
Purple* published in 1982. She is well-known for this quote and others;
visit: https://www.goodreads.com/author/quotes/7380.Alice_Walker

3   For this and other quotes by Maya Angelou, visit: https://www.
goodreads.com/author/quotes/3503.Maya_Angelou

4   Dr. Stan Kutcher is the Sun Life Financial Chair in Adolescent Mental
Health and former director World Health Organization Collaborating
Center in Mental Health Policy and Training at Dalhousie University
and IWK Health Centre in Canada: https://medicine.dal.ca/departments/
department-sites/psychiatry/our-people/faculty/stan-kutcher.html

5   World Health Organization (August 2018). Mental health: Latest
data on suicide. Retrieved December 25, 2018 from https://
www.who.int/mental_health/suicide-prevention/en/

6   Kids Help Phone (2016). One-in-five teens in Canada seriously
considers suicide. https://kidshelpphone.ca/get-involved/
news/one-five-teens-canada-seriously-considers-suicide/

7   Mental Health Commission of Canada (March 2017). Strengthening
the case for investing in Canada's mental health system: Economic
considerations. https://www.mentalhealthcommission.ca/
sites/default/files/2017-03/case_for_investment_eng.pdf

8   For this and other quotes by Marianne Williamson, visit: https://
www.goodreads.com/author/quotes/17297.Marianne_Williamson

9   The Attachment and Trauma Treatment Center for Healing
        informs that the "Window of Tolerance," a term coined by Dr. Dan
        Siegel, is now commonly used to understand and describe normal
        brain/body reactions, especially following adversity. The concept
        suggests that we have an optimal arousal level when we are within
        the window of tolerance that allows for the ebb and flow (ups and
        downs of emotions) experienced by human beings. Learn more
        about Dr. Siegel's work at https://www.drdansiegel.com/

10   *Oh, The Places You'll Go!* (1990), written by Dr. Seuss,
        is a perennial classic for all ages. Find this and his
        other books at http://www.seussville.com/

11   More about Susan Pinker and The Village Effect can be found
        at https://www.susanpinker.com/the-village-effect/

Chapter 2: Taming the Crazy by Getting Crazy

12   Shanker, S. (2016). *Self-Reg: How to Help Your Child
        (and You) Break the Stress Cycle and Successfully
        Engage with Life*. New York: Penguin Press.

13   Stanford Encyclopedia of Philosophy (2015). Behaviorism. From
        https://plato.stanford.edu/entries/behaviorism/#2

14   Stanford Encyclopedia of Philosophy (2015). Behaviorism. From
        https://plato.stanford.edu/entries/behaviorism/#2

15   Stanford Encyclopedia of Philosophy (2015). Behaviorism. From
        https://plato.stanford.edu/entries/behaviorism/#2

16   Robinson, D. (1995). *An Intellectual History of Psychology*.
        Madison, WI: University of Wisconsin Press.

17   Trump, D. (June 20, 2018). Affording Congress an Opportunity to
        Address Family Separation. Whitehouse.gov. July 27, 2018 from https://
        www.whitehouse.gov/presidential-actions/affording-congress-
        opportunity-address-family-separation. Under the Flores Settlement,
        detention of children beyond 20 days has effectively been prohibited

18   Mahatma Gandhi Quotes. Retrieved 2018 from https://www.brainyquote.
        com/authors/mahatma_gandhi. *Young India* was a weekly journal in
        English published by Mohandas Karamchand Gandhi from 1919 to 1931.

19   U.S. Department of Health & Human Services. (n.d.).
      Office of head start: An office of the administration for
      children & families. https://www.acf.hhs.gov/ohs

20   Center on the Developing Child at Harvard University. (2004). Young
      children develop in an environment of relationships: Working
      paper 1. National Scientific Council on the Developing Child. https://
      developingchild.harvard.edu/wp-content/uploads/2004/04/Young-
      Children-Develop-in-an-Environment-of-Relationships.pdf

21   Van Dijken, S. (n.d.). John Bowlby. Encyclopedia Britannica
      https://www.britannica.com/biography/John-Bowlby

22   Winnicott, D.W. (1988). Babies and Their Mothers
      London: Free Association Books.

23   Ainsworth, M. and Bowlby, J. (1965). *Child Care and
      the Growth of Love*. London: Penguin Books.

24   Wikipedia (n.d.). Attachment parenting. http://www.
      wikipedia.org/wiki/Attachment_parenting

25   WebMD (2005-2018). What is attachment parenting? https://www.
      webmd.com/parenting/what-is-attachment-parenting#1

26   For one of many sites about sleep training or cry-it-out
      philosophy, visit: https://www.todaysparent.com/baby/baby-
      sleep/youre-not-evil-if-you-sleep-train-your-baby/

27   To learn more about Dr. Dan Siegel and the upstairs
      brain, visit: https://www.drdansiegel.com/

28   I'm referring here to Habit 5 in: Stephen Covey (1989). *The 7
      Habits of Highly Effective People*. New York: Free Press.

29   Intergenerational trauma is an established psychological concept
      that simply means that the skills one generation has learned about
      coping in life will be passed on to the next generation about how to
      cope in life, and that generation will then pass it on to the following
      generation. Canada's history of Indian Residential Schools is not a
      historical experience, because this and previous generations are still
      coping with the traumatic and harmful experiences suffered in those
      schools. The last federally run Residential School closed in 1996. For
      more information, visit CBC's story A timeline of residential schools,

the Truth and Reconciliation Commission at https://www.cbc.ca/news/
canada/a-timeline-of-residential-schools-the-truth-and-reconciliation-
commission-1.724434. Children and teens who were forced there were
also physically, sexually, and emotionally abused, and the federally-run
schools attempted to commit cultural genocide. These schools were
eventually shut down, but all of those kids (and the kids and teens before
them) were cast back out in the world without corrective experiences
(e.g., counseling, social support, societal inclusion). They moved forward
in the world finding some way to cope but also having relationships,
children, and jobs. For more reading, simply google "Indigenous
intergenerational trauma" or follow the work by Amy Bombay (University
of Ottawa), Kimberly Matheson (Carleton University), Gina Starblanket
(University of Calgary), or Liam Haggarty (Mount Royal University).

30   Greene, R. W. (2014). *Lost at School: Why Our Kids with
Behavior Challenges are Falling through the Cracks
and How We Can Help Them.* New York: Scribner.

31   Circle of Security International: Early Intervention Program for
Parents & Children. https://www.circleofsecurityinternational.
com/books. Hoffman, K., Cooper, G. & Powell, B. (2017). *Raising
a Secure Child: How Circle of Security Parenting Can Help
You Nurture Your Child's Attachment, Emotional Resilience,
and Freedom to Explore.* New York: The Guilford Press.

32   Hoffman, K., Cooper, G. & Powell, B. (2017). *Raising a Secure
Child: How Circle of Security Parenting Can Help You
Nurture Your Child's Attachment, Emotional Resilience, and
Freedom to Explore.* New York: The Guilford Press.

33   The Gottman Institute: A research-based approach to relationships.
(2013). The Research: The Still Face Experiment. https://www.
gottman.com/blog/research-still-face-experiment/

34   Tronik, E. (2007). *Neurobehavioral Social Emotional Development
of Infants and Children.* New York: W.W. Norton & Company.

35   Shanker, S. (2016).

Chapter 3: How I See Them

36   Holmes, J. (1993). *John Bowlby and Attachment
Theory.* New York: Routledge.

37   Mellor, N. (2008). *Attachment Seeking: A Complete Guide for Teachers*. London: SAGE Publications Company.

38   McCloud, C., & Messing, D. (2006). *Have You Filled a Bucket Today: A Guide to Daily Happiness for Kids*. Brighton, MI: Bucket Fillosophy, Bucket Fillers Inc.

39   Moretti, M. & Braber, K. (2013). Connect parent group: An attachment-based treatment manual, revised edition. Simon Fraser University. For more on the amazing parenting program designed for parents of adolescents, visit: http://connectparentgroup.org/

40   American Psychiatric Association. (2013). *Diagnostic and Statistical Manual of Mental Disorders* (5th ed.). Washington, DC: APA Publications.

41   To learn more about learning disabilities, visit: https://ldaamerica.org/types-of-learning-disabilities/ or http://www.acposb.on.ca/conduct-disorder/

42   For more information about ADHD and ADD, visit: https://cmha.bc.ca/documents/attention-deficithyperactivity-disorder-in-adults-2/

43   Ford-Jones, P.C. (2015). Misdiagnosis of Attention-Deficit Hyperactivity Disorder: "Normal behaviour" and relative maturity. Paediatrics & Child Health 20(4): 200–202.

44   For more reading about when brain development ceases, consult Arain, M., Haque, M., Johal, L., Mathur, P., Wynand, N., Rais, A., Sandhu, R., & Sharma, S. (2013). Maturation of the adolescent brain. Journal of Neuropsychiatric Disease & Treatment, 9: 449–461.

45   For more information, visit: https://www.forbes.com/sites/andrewrossow/2018/02/28/cyberbullying-taken-to-a-whole-new-level-enter-the-blue-whale-challenge/#656b4f112673

46   For more details, visit: https://www.imdb.com/title/tt1837492/

47   The Gottman Institute: A research-based approach to relationships. (2013). Marriage and Family. https://www.gottman.com/blog/research-still-face-experiment/. And Gottman, J. (1995). *Why Marriages Succeed or Fail: And How You Can Make Yours Last*. New York: Simon & Schuster.

48   Neufeld, G., & Maté, G. (2013). *Hold On to Your Kids: Why Parents Need to Matter More Than Peers.*. Toronto: Vintage Canada.

49   Wiig, E. H., & Harris, S. P. (1974). Perception and interpretation of nonverbally expressed emotions by adolescents with learning disabilities. Perceptual and Motor Skills, 38(1), 239–245; Arthur, A.R. (2003). The emotional lives of people with learning disability. British Journal of Learning Disabilities, 31(1), 25-30; Mega, C., Ronconi, L., & De Beni, R. (2014). What makes a good student? How emotions, self-regulated learning, and motivation contribute to academic achievement. Journal of Educational Psychology, 106(1), 121-131.

Chapter 4: Trauma Complicates It All

50   Burke Harris, N. (2018). *The Deepest Well: Healing the Long-Term Effects of Childhood Adversity.* New York: Houghton Mifflin Harcourt; van der Kolk, B. (2014).

51   Van der Kolk, B. (2014). *The Body Keeps the Score: Brain, Mind, and Body in the Healing of Trauma.* New York: Gildan Media.

52   Record-Lemon, R. M., & Buchanan, M. J. (2017). Trauma-informed practices in schools: A narrative literature review. Canadian Journal of Counselling and Psychotherapy 51(4), 286-305.

53   For more information, visit: https://education.alberta. ca/trauma-informed-practice/?searchMode=3

54   For more information, visit: https://saferschoolstogether.com/

55   For more information, visit: https://www.nactatr.com/

56   For more information, visit: https://saferschoolstogether. com/ violence-threat-risk-assessment-vtra-protocols-must-be-utilizedto-their-fullest-during-this-extended-critical-period/

57   Craig, S. E. (2016). *Trauma-Sensitive Schools: Learning Communities Transforming Children's Lives, K–5.* New York: Teachers College, Columbia University.

58   Jennings, P.A. (2018). *The Trauma-Sensitive Classroom: Building Resilience with Compassionate Teaching.* New York: W. W. Norton & Company.

59   For more information, visit: http://www.beyondconsequences.com/

60   Sporleder, J., & Forbes, H.T. (2016). *The Trauma-Informed School: A Step-by-Step Implementation Guide for Administrators and School Personnel*. Boulder, CO: Beyond Consequences Institute, LLC.

61   Van der Kolk, B. A. (2002). Trauma and Memory. Psychiatry and Clinical Neurosciences 52(S1).

62   For more information, visit the Alberta Family Wellness Initiative at: https://www.albertafamilywellness.org/what-we-know/aces or http://www.who.int/violence_injury_prevention/violence/activities/adverse_childhood_experiences/en/

63   For more information, visit: https://www.albertafamilywellness.org/faculty-members/vincent-j-felitti

64   Dube, S. R., Anda, R. F., Felitti, V. J., Chapman, D., Williamson, D. F., & Giles, W. H. (2001). Childhood abuse, household dysfunction, and the risk of attempted suicide throughout the life span: Findings from the adverse childhood experiences study. JAMA, 286(24), 3089-3086.

65   Van der Kolk, B. (2014).

66   For more information, visit: https://www.psychiatry.org/patients-families/ptsd/what-is-ptsd

67   Brandt, K., Perry, B.D., Seligman, S., & Tronick, E. (2014). *Infant and Early Childhood Mental Health: Core Concepts and Clinical Practice*. Arlington, VA: American Psychiatric Publishing; Siegel, D. J. & Bryson, T. P. (2012). *The Whole Brain Child: Twelve Revolutionary Strategies to Nurture Your Child's Developing Mind*. New York: Random House Publishing Group; van der Kolk, B. (2014).

68   For information, visit: https://everytown.org/

69   For more information, visit: https://schoolshooters.info/about-dr-langman

70   Porter, S. (1996). Without conscience or without active conscience? The etiology of psychopathy revisited. Aggression and Violent Behavior i(2), 179-189.

71   Jones, A., Sinha, V., & Trocmé, N. (2015). Children and Youth in Out-of-Home Care in the Canadian Provinces. Canadian Child Welfare Research Portal. http://cwrp.ca/sites/default/files/publications/en/167e.pdf

72   For more information, visit https://www.gov.mb.ca/fs/

73   Government of Canada. First Nations Child and Family Services. Retrieved December 26, 2018 from https://www.sac-isc.gc.ca/eng/1100100035204/1533307858805

74   Sinclair, R. (2007). Identity lost and found: Lessons from the sixties scoop. The First People's Child and Family Review, 3(1), 10-15.

75   For more information about the Ministerial Panel, their multi-phase study, and recommendations, visit: https://www.alberta.ca/child-intervention-panel.x?fbclid=IwAR0wqTKKNi3FtG2jXm h3CoH4VtXlo4LUsids52TCaqs9mUBgTeODHs7ObM and https://open.alberta.ca/dataset/bb927d32-61da-4014-82b2-1746ac26e88f/resource/8e03a767-f579-4014-a9ab-4a4373f1b89e/download/mpci-recommendations-to-minister-of-childrens-services.pdf

76   U.S. Department of Health and Human Services, Administration for Children and Families, Administration on Children, Youth and Families, Children's Bureau. (2017). The AFCARS Report. https://www.acf.hhs.gov/sites/default/files/cb/afcarsreport24.pdf

77   Blodgett, C., & Dorado, J. (2015). A Selected Review of Trauma-Informed School Practice and Alignment with Educational Practice. https://s3.wp.wsu.edu/uploads/sites/2101/2015/02/CLEAR-Trauma-Informed-Schools-White-Paper.pdf

78   For this and other quotes by Peter A. Levine, visit: https://www.goodreads.com/author/quotes/142956.Peter_A_Levine

Chapter 5: Grief

79   Owens, D. (2008). Recognizing the needs of bereaved children in palliative care. Journal of Hospice & Palliative Nursing 10(1), 14-16.

80   To learn more about Dr. Elisabeth Kübler-Ross and the Elisabeth Kübler-Ross Foundation, visit: https://www.ekrfoundation.org/

81   To learn more about Dr. Brené Brown, visit: https://brenebrown.com/

82   To learn more about Dr. Alan Wolfelt and the Center for Loss
      & Life Transition, visit: https://www.centerforloss.com/

83   For more information about author Mitch Albom and
      his books, visit: https://www.mitchalbom.com/

Chapter 6: The Answer: Getting Hearts and Taking Names
84   Siegel, D. J. & Bryson, T. P. (2012).

Chapter 7: The Carrington Connections Network for Educators
85   Dalio, R. (2017). *Principles: Life and Work*. New York: Simon & Schuster.

86   Brown, B. (2018). *Dare to Lead: Brave Work. Tough
      Conversations. Whole Hearts.*. New York: Random House.

87   To learn more about Jimmy Casas and J Casas and
      Associates, visit: https://jimmycasas.com/

88   College of Alberta Superintendents, November 2018.

89   National Center for Education Statistics; Association for
      Supervision and Curriculum Development; and American
      Association of School Administrators, the State of the American
      School Superintendency: A Mid-Decade Survey).

90   For more information about the Children's First Act,
      visit: https://www.aheaonline.com/political-updates/
      children-first-act-albertas-childrens-charter

91   Casas, J. (2017). *Culturize: Every Student. Every Day. Whatever
      It Takes*. San Diego, CA: Dave Burgess Consulting, Inc.

92   For more information, visit: https://www.leaderinme.org/

93   For more information, visit: https://saferschoolstogether.com/
      violence-threat-risk-assessment-vtra-protocols-must-be-utilized-
      to-their-fullest-during-this-extended-critical-period/

94   For more information, visit: http://www.
      zonesofregulation.com/index.html

95   For more information, visit: https://jigsawlearning.
      ca/category/collaborative-response-model/

Chapter 8: The Kids Are the Least of Our Worries

96   Alberta School Employee Benefit Plan (2017). Your Companion in Health: We are ASEBP 2017 Annual Report. https://www.asebp. ca/sites/default/files/forms/2017_ASEBP_Annual_Report.pdf

97   Cassa, 2017.

98   Kids Help Phone data, 2017.

99   To learn more about Dr. Charles Figley or compassion fatigue, visit: https://charlesfigley.com/

100   To learn more about Dr. Gabor Maté, visit: https://drgabormate.com/

101   For this quote and others by L.R. Knost, visit: https://www. goodreads.com/author/quotes/5116439.L_R_Knost

102   Clance, P. R., & Imes, S. A. (1978). The imposter phenomenon in high achieving women: Dynamics and therapeutic intervention. Psychotherapy: Theory, Research & Practice 15(3), 241-247.

103   To learn more about Dr. Robert D. Enright and the International Forgiveness Institute, visit: https://internationalforgiveness.com/

104   Worthington, E. J., & Scherer, M. (2004). Forgiveness is an emotion-focused coping strategy that can reduce health risks and promote health resilience: Theory, review and hypotheses. Journal of Psychology and Health 19(3) 385.

105   Toussaint, L. L., Worthington, E. L., & Williams, D. R. (Eds.) *Forgiveness and Health: Scientific Evidence and Theories Relating Forgiveness to Better Health*. New York, NY: Springer Science and Business Media.

106   Lerner, H. (2017). *Why Won't You Apologize: Healing Big Betrayals and Everyday Hurts*. New York: Simon & Schuster.

107   For more information about collective effervescence and Émile Durkheim, visit http://www.wikiwand.com/en/Collective_effervescence

108   To learn more about this concept and about Chrissy Powers, visit: https://chrissypowers.com/people-hard-hate-close-move/

109   Sandberg, S. (2013). *Lean In: Women, Work, and the Will to Lead*. New York: Albert A. Knopf and the Lean-In Foundation.

110   Sandberg, S. (2017). *Option B: Facing Adversity, Building Resilience, and Finding Joy.* New York: Albert A. Knopf and OptionB.org.

INDEX

More from

IMPRESS

Empower
What Happens When Students Own Their Learning
A.J. Juliani and John Spencer

In an ever-changing world, educators and parents must take a role in helping students prepare themselves for **anything**. That means unleashing their creative potential! In **Empower**, A.J. Juliani and John Spencer provide teachers, coaches, and administrators with a roadmap that will inspire innovation, authentic learning experiences, and practical ways to empower students to pursue their passions while in school.

Learner-Centered Innovation
Spark Curiosity, Ignite Passion, and Unleash Genius
Katie Martin

Learning opportunities and teaching methods **must** evolve to match the ever-changing needs of today's learners. In **Learner-Centered Innovation**, Katie Martin offers insights into how to make the necessary shifts and create an environment where learners at every level are empowered to take risks in pursuit of learning and growth rather than perfection.

Unleash Talent
Bringing Out the Best in Yourself and the Learners You Serve
Kara Knollmeyer

In **Unleash Talent**, educator and principal Kara Knollmeyer explains that by exploring the core elements of talent—passion, skills, and personality traits—you can uncover your gifts and help others do the same. Whether you are a teacher, administrator, or custodian, this insightful guide will empower you to use your unique talents to make a powerful impact on your school community.

Reclaiming Our Calling
Hold on to the Heart, Mind, and Hope of Education
Brad Gustafson

Children are more thazn numbers, and we are called to teach and reach them accordingly. In this genre-busting book, award-winning educator and principal Brad Gustafson uses stories to capture the heart, mind, and hope of education.

Take the L.E.A.P
Ignite a Culture of Innovation
Elisabeth Bostwick

Take the L.E.A.P.: Ignite a Culture of Innovation will inspire and support you as you to take steps to grow beyond traditional and self-imposed boundaries. Award-winning educator Elisabeth Bostwick shares stories and practical strategies to help you challenge conventional thinking and create the conditions that empower meaningful learning.

Drawn to Teach
An Illustrated Guide to Transforming Your Teaching
Josh Stumpenhorst, Illustrated by Trevor Guthke

If you're looking for ways to help your students succeed, you won't find the answer in gimmicks, trends, or fads. Great teaching isn't about test results or data; it's about connecting with students and empowering them to own their learning. Through this clever, illustrated guide, Josh Stumpenhorst reveals the key characteristics all top educators share in common and shows you how to implement them in your teaching practice.

Math Recess
Playful Learning in an Age of Disruption
Sunil Singh and Dr. Christopher Brownell

In the theme of recess, where a treasure chest of balls, ropes, and toys would be kept for children to play with, this book holds a deep and imaginative collection of fun mathematical ideas, puzzles, and problems. Written for anyone interested in or actively engaged in schools– parents, teachers, administrators, school board members–this book shows math as a playful, fun, and wonderfully human activity that everyone can enjoy... for a lifetime!

Innovate Inside the Box
Empowering Learners Through UDL and Innovator's Mindset
George Couros

In *Innovate Inside the Box,* George Couros and Katie Novak provide informed insight on creating purposeful learning opportunities for all students. By combining the power of the Innovator's Mindset and Universal Design for Learning (UDL), they empower educators to create opportunities that will benefit every learner.

Personal & Authentic
Designing Learning Experiences That Impact a Lifetime
Thomas C. Murray

In *Personal & Authentic*, Thomas C. Murray reveals the power of designing awe-inspiring experiences that are grounded in relationships and learner-centered by design. Inherently relevant and contextualized, it is this kind of learning that lasts a lifetime.

CPSIA information can be obtained
at www.ICGtesting.com
Printed in the USA
LVHW012040220221
679615LV00005BA/811